EDUCATIONAL
DISOBEDIENCE

EDUCATIONAL DISOBEDIENCE

A Mom Who Became A Movement

DR. ANNISE MABRY

Copyright © 2024 by Dr. Annise Mabry Foundation

All rights reserved. No part of this book may be reproduced in any form, except as applied to brief quotations incorporated into critical articles or reviews.

The information provided in this book is designed to provide helpful information on the subjects discussed. The author is not offering it as legal or other professional services advice. Although the author has made every effort to ensure that the information in this book was correct at press time, the author shall not be held liable or responsible to any person or entity with respect to any loss or incidental or consequential damages caused, or alleged to have been caused, directly or indirectly, by the information contained herein.

Cover Designer: Fahi M.

Interior Design: Creative Publishing Book Design

ISBN Paperback: 978-1-7324966-1-3

To my children Niles and Emmett—it is an honor to be your mom. Your determination, strength, and boundless potential are my greatest inspirations. Continue challenging the status quo in the world. Always forge your own path with courage and wisdom.

Love, Mom

Contents

Introduction: Unraveling the Notion of Educational Disobedience 1

Chapter 1: The Original Educational Disruptor 5

Chapter Two: Humble Beginnings 9

Chapter Three: Ripple Effects 15

Chapter Four: The First Year 23

Chapter Five: Homeschool Not Aloneschool 35

Chapter Six: Homeschooling With an IEP 43

Chapter Seven: The Tiers Free Model 51

Chapter Eight: The First Graduation 56

Chapter Nine: Trauma-Informed Academic Program 62

Chapter Ten: The Movement 65

Chapter Eleven: Macon County Chiefs' Diploma Program 71

    Epilogue 78

Appendix A: In Their Own Words 82

    Emmett's Story 83

    2019 Brandilyn Cromer "Thrive with Pride" 86

    2020 Jessica Stephens "My High School Journey" 87

    2020 Katiesha Tiera Smith 91

    2020 Brittney Marjorie Powell 92

    2021 Rachel Wall 94

2021 Stephanie Johnson 96

2022 Jessica Stewart 98

2022 Deneen Evette Porter 100

2022 John Andrades Baisden 103

2022 Shentoria Baisden 105

2022 Rashad Jones "My Journey to a High School Diploma" 107

2022 Michael Lynn McGhee Jr. 109

2023 Guadalupe Benitez Paredes 113

2023 Tiara Holmes "Foster Care Is Failing but I'm Graduating" 115

2023 Travis Fudge 119

2023 Jennika Harris 121

2023 Keyoshia Sanders 123

2024 Joy Green "Hidden Homelessness: Rising Above" 126

2024 Brian Young 128

2024 Sir David Elijah Patrick Byron-Dodson 130

2024 Alexa Pulido 132

2024 Elijah Weston-Vaughn 134

2024 Cassius Bell 137

2024 Brittany Myers 139

2024 Jasmine Bivins 141

2024 Dottie 144

Crystal Spence, Parent Reflection of Program Impact 146

2024 Kaylin Driggers 148

Appendix B: Homeschool Pro Tips: The Stuff I Wish I Knew When I Started 152

    Homeschool Pro Tip: Position for a learning pivot. 152

    Homeschool Pro Tip: Build learning confidence first. Focus on content mastery second. 153

    Homeschool Pro Tip: Design your own student support team. 153

    Homeschool Pro Tip: Buy used curriculum. 154

    Homeschool Pro Tip: Leverage dual enrollment classes for high school students. 154

    Homeschool Pro Tip: Facilitate learning that fosters independence. 155

    Homeschool Pro Tip: Keep all of your records. 155

Appendix C: The Plain Language Homeschool Checklist 157

    Pre-Decision Checklist. 157

    Planning and Preparation. 158

    Implementation 159

    Ongoing Support and Growth 160

    Acknowledgements 161

INTRODUCTION
Unraveling the Notion of Educational Disobedience

In the realm of education, conformity has long been championed as the cornerstone of success: a system designed to mold young minds into compliant citizens, fitting neatly into predetermined societal roles. However, amidst the structured corridors of traditional learning, there exists a disruptive force—one that challenges the status quo, dares to question authority, and advocates for a different kind of education. This force is none other than "Educational Disobedience."

It is true that a single spark can transform an entire landscape. I became that spark for education reform and change in my community as I dared to leverage homeschool laws to weave a safety net for my children, who were first left behind and later educationally excluded from traditional learning environments. I could not allow my children to fail. The educational safety net I wove to save them evolved into a bridge that now transforms over four hundred high school dropouts into high school graduates each year. Forty-six percent of the graduates from my homeschool cooperative not only enroll in technical and community colleges within three months of graduation, but they also complete their degree programs, with many students making the Dean's List. In 2024, the neighborhood homeschool cooperative I built to educate my own children issued its one thousandth homeschool high school diploma.

Tiers Free Academy Homeschool Cooperative, a program under The Dr. Annise Mabry Foundation, is the only homeschool cooperative in Georgia that receives grant funding as a United Way Learning Loss Service Provider to serve seventy-eight rural, persistent poverty communities with some of the lowest graduation rates in Georgia. This achievement is significant because it enables me to collaborate with school districts, offering direct services to families and students who urgently need alternative educational programs but face financial barriers. This partnership is particularly vital because my student population defies the conventional image of homeschool students, encompassing diverse racial and socioeconomic backgrounds.

I had never realized that entire families could go through generations without ever experiencing the sense of fulfillment that comes from watching a child cross the stage and transform from high school student to high school graduate. Many were trapped in never- ending cycles of adult literacy programs that didn't understand the populations they served and therefore, failed to meet their needs. I understood this population because I was part of it.

My childhood friend DeeDee Hill once told me, "Programs created outside the hood can't save the hood. Only the hood can save the hood." I didn't fully grasp DeeDee's words until I encountered these programs firsthand. It became clear that you can't effectively assist a population with a problem you haven't personally experienced or deeply understood. I get it now.

The concept of Educational Disobedience is as multifaceted as it is provocative. It encompasses a range of actions, attitudes, and philosophies that diverge from the mainstream educational narrative.

I was the parent of two special-needs children who were six years apart in age with very different learning styles and abilities. I knew from my own children that a one-size-fits-all approach wasn't going to work. Educational Disobedience is a rebellion against the rigidity of conventional schooling.

At its core, Educational Disobedience is a rallying cry for autonomy, critical thinking, and innovation in education. It refuses to accept knowledge as a static entity to be passively absorbed but instead sees learning as a dynamic, participatory process. It rejects the notion that success can be measured solely by standardized tests and grades, advocating for a more holistic, student-centric approach that values creativity, curiosity, and individuality.

Educational Disobedience is not my story alone. It's the story of all of those who heard my battle cry and made the choice to embark on a journey to unravel the complexities of modern education, transform what homeschooling truly means, and imagine a more liberated, empowering future.

I want to take you on a journey that will illuminate how it felt to be an educator who dared to challenge the status quo. I'd like to tell you the stories of students who defied expectations, and ultimately, about a movement that reduced the crime rate from 69 percent to 13 percent in one community, increased the high school graduation rate of an entire school district from 70 percent to 90 percent, and transformed communities while revolutionizing the way we think about learning. In the chapters that follow, I will confront uncomfortable truths about the limitations of traditional education and explore alternative models that prioritize student empowerment. Ultimately, this exploration is not just an academic exercise but a call to action. I want you to question your own assumptions about education, to challenge oppressive systems, and to imagine new possibilities for teaching and learning. If you are a parent fighting to save your child, an aunt fighting to save your niece or nephew, or an educator who is tired of fighting the system—I see you because I have been you.

I was the educator who was essentially terminated from her position because I dared to speak out against for-profit universities preying on first-generation minority students. I was the parent who was told in one breath that my child was academically gifted but also that I needed to "come pick your child up, never bring your child back, this isn't working for us" when she didn't fit the mold of what a gifted child should do. I was the parent who had an investigation opened against her for educational neglect because I refused to send my autistic child back into a learning environment that didn't have the resources I knew he needed to succeed.

I didn't become educationally disobedient by choice—I became disobedient because my children would not have survived had I remained silent.

As we navigate this terrain of dissent and disruption, let us remember the words of Paulo Freire, who famously declared, "There is no such thing as a neutral education process. Education either functions as an instrument to bring about conformity or freedom." With Educational Disobedience, we choose the path of freedom.

1

The Original Educational Disruptor

Inherently independent, I thrived on self-reliance, believing my traits and achievements were entirely self-made. My beliefs, standards, and the path I meticulously carved seemed rooted solely in my own efforts. Then, one Sunday afternoon, my mother sat me down and unveiled the story of my grandfather. As I absorbed this revelation, stunned by a family history kept hidden from me all these years, I realized in an instant that the essence of my spirit and purpose had been shaped long before my own existence began.

It was the 1940s in Carroll County, Georgia and my grandfather was the child of a bi-racial relationship—a relationship that was illegal because my great-grandmother was born into slavery. She continued to work at the plantation where she had been a slave until my grandfather was a teenager.

My grandfather grew up during an era when teaching Blacks to read and write was downright dangerous. He was given an opportunity to learn because he passed as white. Passing is a concept with deep historical roots, particularly in the United States, where individuals of mixed race, especially African Americans, would present themselves as white to avoid racial segregation and discrimination. I have some experience with this too because as a feminine-presenting African American lesbian, I often rely on the ability to blend in when I'm in public or unsure about the safety of my surroundings. I imagine my grandfather felt much the same way.

When my grandfather married my grandmother, his ability to pass became limited in many situations. So, he gravitated more to the Black community where my grandmother was accepted. In the 1940s, they lived in an area with other Black sharecroppers, but my grandfather was the only sharecropper who could read and write.

My grandmother knew how dangerous this was for him and their family so she frequently discouraged him from making this fact public knowledge. I grew up hearing my mom say, "Never let your right hand know what your left hand is doing." As a kid, I learned this meant to keep secrets. As an adult, I realize this was the passage of generational trauma.

The turning point for my grandfather came during one harvest season when he watched so many sharecroppers being cheated out of profits that were rightfully theirs. My grandmother begged him not to challenge the status quo but my grandfather knew an injustice when he saw it, and this time he leveraged his passing privilege to change it. One by one, my grandfather began teaching the Black sharecroppers how to read, write, and count their money. He explained what working on halves truly meant and showed them how to sell some of their harvest on their own instead of turning everything over to the land owner.

This bold move made not only my grandfather a target but also his entire family. One day while my grandmother was cleaning houses, she got word that the Ku Klux Klan was gathering to teach my grandfather a lesson because one of the sharecroppers my grandfather taught had stood up to the landowner. At first, when the landowner asked the sharecropper how he had learned these new skills, he was silent, but he finally gave up my grandfather's name.

My grandmother left work early that day to go find my grandfather. As they slowly realized what was about to happen, my grandfather began formulating a plan to get his family out of town. It wasn't going to be easy, especially since they were now being watched. The next day, no one left that three-room house, and my grandmother spent all day baking what little food they had and packing what they could fit into a wagon with eight children.

Finally, the early morning hours fell and my grandfather began loading his children into the wagon one at a time. The oldest children went on first and were told to lie flat and be still. My grandfather had bored tiny holes in the sides of the wagon so they could breathe. Then the younger children were loaded into the wagon and a roughly constructed flat board was placed over them. Furniture was placed on top of the board and my grandfather then covered the entire wagon in a sheet that my grandmother had sewn.

This was their survival ride. There were no goodbyes to the neighbors with whom they had built relationships over the years because the smallest amount of information leaked at the wrong time to the wrong person could result in death.

My mom often recounts being on that wagon as the dark night turned to morning and then finally a full day when the wagon stopped.

As my grandfather unloaded the wagon at their new home, he gave the children strict instructions to never talk about where they came from, how they had arrived, and especially to never mention any names of their old neighbors.

What impressed me most was that my grandfather never stopped teaching. He just learned how to be more discerning about who he taught and how much he taught them.

My grandfather passed away forty years ago and I never got to learn all of this family history from him. But one thing my mom always instilled in me was the importance of education. Only in the last decade have I been able to connect the dots.

Sometimes, as I navigate the familiar dirt roads of my rural roots, thoughts of my grandfather inevitably flood my mind. It saddens me that his story, so intimately intertwined with mine, was relayed to me by my mother after he passed. I find myself yearning to converse with him, to ask the countless questions that linger unspoken. I feel a profound connection to him, as if I've inherited his legacy—a guiding force that manifests itself when I witness someone transforming their life from dropout to high school graduate with my support. Or, when I found myself at a crossroads and took the courageous steps to challenge and reshape the traditional boundaries of our educational system.

2
Humble Beginnings

In the summer of 1995, I wandered the echoing hallways of the East Point Police Department, a novice in the realm of law enforcement. The sharp scent of freshly polished floors mixed with the low hum of radios and murmurs of busy officers was both thrilling and over whelming. My uniform, heavy on my shoulders, felt like a mantle of responsibility, a promise of commitment and duty. I embraced my role despite the challenges, working through the adrenaline from responding to calls and enduring the trauma of what I witnessed. Life as a police officer wasn't exactly as I had imagined it. Yet life, in its unrelenting manner, threw me a curveball just a year later.

By 1996, I found myself at the Luthersville Police Department, stepping into a new role with a mixture of excitement and uncertainty. It was a new chapter in my rapidly shifting story. My yearning for a broader spectrum of experiences led me to a part-time gig as a 911 dispatcher with Coweta County Emergency Management Services. My evenings were spent in the dim glow of dispatch screens, fielding calls that ranged from the mundane to the life-threatening.

The whirlwind continued into the next year as I juggled multiple roles—an unexpected challenge I embraced with determination. I took on a part-time position as a Communications Intern at

Georgia Pacific, dived into corporate communications, and began instructing adults in literacy at Literacy Action. My days became a frenetic mix of public safety, corporate memos, and teaching.

In 1998, I found myself once again navigating a whirlwind of new experiences. I became a law enforcement wife and a mom. I was entering my third new career in four years. I applied for graduate school despite the objections of my husband, who wanted me to hurry up and graduate from college so I could simply work and take care of my child. My career path no longer felt fitting. I couldn't explain it but I knew I had a purpose that far exceeded my current circumstances.

It seemed like everyone in my life, in the hope that I would find some career stability, was pushing me to enter the new Teacher Alternative Program (TAP). TAP allowed people with degrees in fields other than education an opportunity to explore teaching as a career. In truth, it was the last thing I ever dreamed of doing. I had no desire to teach anyone anything for any reason. What I did know was that with my new role as a mother, flexibility was a top priority. Being married to a police officer felt like I was raising my child as a single parent.

One afternoon, my neighbor knocked on my front door. She asked if I would be interested in a two-week substitute position at the local elementary school, and I quickly gave her all the reasons why I couldn't—even down to my lack of a degree in education. My neighbor was persuasive, persistent, and supportive. I conceded solely because we needed the money.

I submitted my application on a Friday morning and by lunch on the following Monday, I was sitting in an eight-hour substitute teaching training session. Seventy-two hours later, I found myself in a classroom with twenty-two third-graders who were just one month into their school year while I was their fourth substitute teacher, which shocked me. After their regular teacher returned, I continued to accept long-term substitute assignments.

The previous years I had spent as a law enforcement officer stuck with me. You can walk away from the job, but you can never shake off the training—it embeds itself deep within you. When I stepped into the classroom as a substitute teacher, I didn't approach it with the mindset of an educator; instead, I carried the ingrained instincts and experiences of a traumatized police officer.

I was the teacher who insisted on locking classroom doors while others propped them open for convenience during recess. My colleagues often teased me, calling me paranoid.

"We're in an elementary school," they'd say. "There's no danger here like in high schools. You're overreacting." But it wasn't just paranoia. Somehow, I sensed that the tragedy at Columbine in April 1999 would permanently alter the experience of attending school.

I felt an urgent need to foster community in my classroom. Beyond the lesson plans, I wanted to create a safe space where my students could experience the essence of learning together, and I taught them the importance of looking out for one another. In our classroom, we weren't twenty-three individuals but a single cohesive unit.

While bullying wasn't new, post-Columbine it gained heightened awareness, prompting educators to be vigilant for potential victims. In response, my class was unique; we operated in pairs, a deliberate choice I made when arranging seating. I intentionally paired students of different backgrounds, emphasizing that together, we were stronger than our individual differences.

I made it my mission to ensure that my students never went home and said, "I was bullied today" or "I had to eat alone because no one wanted to eat lunch with me."

Call it first-year teacher optimism, but I believed that if I took a proactive stance on addressing the classroom bullying before it started, then I could somehow create a butterfly effect within the education system. I had always believed that the public educational system would work. I believed that it operated and was executed well from the student-centric perspective and that issues with bullying could be easily resolved by simply maintaining an adult presence.

In 2001, I leaped further into the world of academia by accepting a position as an adjunct professor at DeVry University, all while celebrating my graduation with an Executive MBA in Business Communications. Unbeknownst to me at the time, that year marked the beginning of a profound journey, which would see me earn a Master's in Adult Education and Distance Learning by 2004. By 2005, I embraced a full-time role as an online faculty trainer at DeVry University Online, immersing myself in the evolving world of digital education. Yet, amid my professional ascent, my personal life took a dramatic turn; in 2008, I faced the end of my marriage.

The turbulence of that year and the struggles in my personal life only fueled my ambition, and in 2009, I was honored with a promotion to Dean of Graduate Studies, a role that underscored my perseverance and dedication in the ever-evolving landscape of higher education.

The promotion was not merely a step up the ladder; it was a testament to the resilience and adaptability I had developed over the years. The role brought with it a host of responsibilities—overseeing graduate programs, shaping academic policies, and mentoring students and faculty alike. It was a position that demanded both vision and practical skills, and I embraced it with a renewed sense of purpose.

I wish I can say it was all roses, but it turned out to be the exact opposite. In retrospect, neither my ex-husband nor I was fully prepared to balance the demands of our careers with the responsibilities of parenting. We were so consumed with chasing an elusive version of the American Dream that the sacrifices required for parenthood became almost insurmountable. For me, that pursuit, especially as a Black woman, evolved into a disheartening reality—a pursuit that ultimately, became a nightmare.

Academia, in many ways, failed me and countless others like me. I speak with a raw honesty that transcends casual conversations and confronts the harsh truth: microaggressions were the norm, and an unspoken rule dictated that I was to be the first in and the last out, the last to be promoted and the first to be let go. I wore my underrepresentation like a badge of honor, a false symbol of arrival when, in reality, I was being tokenized. I understood this even then, but voicing it felt like a betrayal of a dream I was still clinging to.

Despite the hard work, the systemic inequities remained inescapable. I authored a dissertation on preparing online faculty to engage underprepared learners, but the support from my university was nonexistent. They were quick to showcase my work at distance education conferences yet failed to acknowledge my efforts in any meaningful way. My dedication to the field only highlighted the futility of trying to overcome a system that was comfortable with unequal burdens and expectations.

One particularly telling year, I was tasked with constructing the graduate class schedule—a responsibility previously handled collaboratively by the registrar, a graduate assistant, and the graduate dean. Now, it was solely my job. Meanwhile, a white female dean had her team develop her schedule, which was then reviewed side-by-side with mine. This stark contrast underscored the inequities that plagued my role.

Sitting in the so-called ivory tower, I accepted this toxic reality as my own. It bred a deep-seated trauma that only recently has started to receive the attention it deserves. When I share my experiences, I often say, "I was the first Black, openly lesbian Dean of Graduate Studies at one of the largest for-profit universities. For anyone who is BIPOC and LGBTQ+ entering academia, I have come to believe three crucial truths: The expectations and demands placed upon you will differ starkly from those placed on your non-minority colleagues. You will be expected to deliver more with fewer resources. And, tragically, you will often be the last to be promoted and the first to be downsized." My academic journey, once filled with aspirations of stability and success, became fraught with challenges. I remember my excitement when I landed my first job as an adjunct online professor in 1999. My small office, the weekly student recruitment meetings, and the balancing act of parenting and career were all part of this dream. Yet the reality of academia, particularly for Black women like me, took a toll on my marriage, my children, and even my health. I knew I would not be able to sustain it much longer.

3

Ripple Effects

Little did I anticipate how much the educational landscape would transform between the time I taught the elementary class in 1999 and my daughter's sixth-grade year in 2010. Considering the rapid technological advancements of the early 2000s, ten years in education felt like an entire generational shift.

As my children grew, I taught them the same principles I instilled in my classroom ten years prior. My morning mantra to them each day was, "Work within the system. Follow the chain of command. Never throw the first punch."

My daughter was a child who loved learning. In kindergarten, she was reading chapter books, while by fifth grade, she was reading and comprehending at the college level. Yet she never tested into the gifted program, as each year she would miss entrance by one or two points. This is the same child who would later enter college as a dual enrollment student at fifteen. Had I allowed my child to believe what the public school system was telling her, she would have internalized the message that she wasn't smart enough to go after the opportunity to become a dual enrollment student, let alone obtain sixty college credits by her seventeenth birthday.

Educational bias is real. Not only am I observing it now as a parent, but I also noticed it when I was teaching. At the school where I worked, some parents were allowed to choose their child's teacher, while others had no such privilege. The administrator who had publicly praised all teachers as equally qualified assured us that parental influence would not affect class assignments. However, it soon became clear that assignments were determined by which parents requested which teachers and which ones were less likely to complain. Additionally, families from certain zip codes had more influence in this process. Not only was this disheartening, but it killed the morale and camaraderie between teachers.

On the other side of the coin, as a parent, I saw the bias in certain kids' access to the gifted program. These children got to take extra field trips and participate in exciting learning activities. Every child in my daughter's school wanted to be in the gifted program, but each grade level had only ten slots, for a total of fifty exceptionally gifted students.

I was also astutely aware of the educational privilege my children received simply because of our address, zip code, and those two letters (Dr.) in front of my name. There is a seldom discussed housing bias in education, established by parents who move into certain neighbor- hoods to "eliminate" undesirable elements in the classroom. These same parents become very upset when apartments or condos are built in their communities, because they see the families who move into those neighborhoods as a transient population coming purposefully to take advantage of the available resources—especially the educational resources—without putting back into the community.

I was one of those parents who selected school districts by their test scores. When we lived in one subdivision of Atlanta, Georgia in 2002, the starting price of homes was $225,000. This was the price point the developers knew they needed in order to build their picture-perfect neighborhood without specifically stating who they wanted to reside there. The city was tasked with creating more affordable housing, so their idea was to put developer-built condos with a starting price of $150,000 into the neighborhood. I recall the venom that spewed from the mouths of the existing homeowners as they shared their irrational fears of how the condo residents would adversely impact property values and classroom sizes.

From my daughter's perspective, the first time she experienced educational bias was in kindergarten. Because I was enrolled in the graduate education program, I had access to a wide array of standardized gifted student exams used by school districts and educational consultants to evaluate students for the gifted program. When I recommended my daughter for gifted evaluation at the end of her first semester, I was met with an immediate wall of academic resistance. Rather than back down, I kept pushing, partly because I had administered four different tests and on all of them, she scored in the range of an academically gifted student who needed intellectual challenges.

What I didn't realize is that my push for her to be included into the program was actually making her a target; even her smallest missteps were magnified, and she was often excluded more than included. My daughter was ultimately being used as a pawn in a fight she didn't even start because people in leadership didn't feel like she belonged. It was her kindergarten teacher who finally found the courage to speak up, and she independently scored her. The teacher's gifted score was only one point off in the exact same area I had scored. Even still, my daughter never got into the gifted program in that school district. This journey taught me two valuable lessons about advocating for my child's education: Be prepared to play the long game, and be ready for unintentional collateral damage.

For years, my daughter begged me to homeschool her; time and again, I found a reason for why it wasn't a good idea. I made so many excuses. But the truth was, despite being a trained teacher, the prospect of being 100 percent responsible for my daughter's education terrified me. It terrified me because I knew some homeschool parents and I was nothing like them. The moms in these families were true stay-at-home moms. I didn't see any working moms or single moms homeschooling. I didn't see any moms going to college and homeschooling. And I definitely didn't see any moms like me homeschooling. There was no representation of me anywhere. When I looked around my suburban $250K house on the lake and golf course community, I saw no representation of anyone who looked like me, and I wouldn't have had anything to use as my success metric to even know if I was doing it right.

But rather than try to explain all of this to an elementary child, I made excuses such as, "I have to work full-time and you are too young to manage the work alone"; "I don't have time to do all those homeschool field trips"; "You'll miss out on the socialization of school." My experience and academic training led me to believe that public education at the hands of complete strangers was a better option than me teaching my own child. The irony was that my own daughter believed more in me and my ability to homeschool her than I did myself. After my daughter completed her first year of middle school, we moved to a new county. This left us without the support network we had in our previous location, creating the perfect storm for difficulties.

When she finally confided that she was being bullied, we promptly sought help from the school administration. Her sexual orientation was one factor fueling the bullying; she had openly shared with me in late elementary school that she was a lesbian. I had always believed in the fluidity of sexuality and met her coming out with celebration. However, her journey intensified the strain on my already crumbling marriage. I was determined to create a safe space for her, unlike the acceptance for which I struggled after coming out at sixteen, being kicked out at seventeen, and eventually succumbing to my mother's attempts to "pray away the gay" to fit back into my family.

When we relocated, my daughter began to identify as transgender, which only exacerbated the bullying. She faced not only peer bullying but also discrimination from adults in positions of authority who were uncomfortable with her gender expression. Their reluctance to act only worsened the situation, and my hesitation to homeschool her left her vulnerable to what our school superintendent later described as "one of the most extreme cases" of bullying ever encountered in the county. In an ideal world, once the administration had become aware, they would have taken steps to protect my daughter and to correct the behaviors of the bullies. Sadly, that didn't happen, partly because in 2009, the antibullying policies on the books in our county hadn't been updated since the 1980s. We were facing new age bullies with outdated policies, and the administration found themselves unprepared to manage this crisis.

The bullies got bolder; they stabbed her with pencils, hit her in the back of the head with literature books, and spat in her food at lunch. Her only safe place to eat was the bathroom.

Each time she tried to report the assaults, the administration insisted they couldn't act because they hadn't witnessed the incidents firsthand. But the bullying didn't stop at physical attacks; it soon extended to taunting online. My initial response was to advise her to simply avoid social media, thinking it would solve the problem. However, in 2009, social media was just beginning to take hold; Facebook had only recently opened its doors to non-college students in 2006, and the iPhone was barely two years old. I hadn't grasped that social media was becoming the primary way for her generation to socialize and connect. My advice to stay away from it was misguided—why should my child be cut off from the very platform that was her main avenue for social interaction?

My daughter's spirit broke. She became angry at everything and everyone. She was the victim, yet I was telling her to change her behavior as if she were the perpetrator. Even a simple request such as "Please turn the light off" gave way to a major battle with her. All of the rage that my daughter had bottled up had to come out somewhere, and I bore the brunt of it.

Overnight, I transformed in my daughter's eyes from her greatest ally to her number-one enemy. What I failed to realize at the time was that her anger about being bullied was spilling over and affecting everyone around us—from our household to my relationships with close family friends. We were all caught in the wake of the bullying. The situation reached a breaking point when my daughter—who had never been in trouble before—was suspended three times in just thirty days. With each suspension, her anger intensified, and I shared in that frustration. Despite my experience as an educator and law enforcement official, I felt powerless to protect my own child.

When I asked for the opportunity to use the hospital homebound services for the remaining sixty days of my daughter's school year, the county educational services coordinator said, "Hospital homebound services are for medically fragile children only. I cannot waste those resources on a child that is not medically fragile."

I was stunned; I couldn't imagine a child more emotionally fragile than one who had faced relentless bullying, attempted suicide thirteen times in a year, and received no safe learning environment from the very adults entrusted with her education. Despite this, I persisted, and she was eventually granted hospital homebound services for the rest of the school year. When I learned that Karen Ravenell-Meertins had been assigned as our homebound teacher, I felt an immense academic burden lift. It wasn't because I knew anything about her, but because I was exhausted and in dire need of support. Karen symbolized the help we desperately required.

To my relief, Karen proved to be exceptional at handling my daughter's unpredictable mood swings. While my daughter thrived academically, her emotional struggles persisted. The harsh truth was that the intervention came too late. The weeks and months I had spent battling with the administration to shield her from the bullies amounted to lost time. I now regret not recognizing sooner that the school system was fundamentally powerless to protect my child.

My daughter was deeply traumatized, and she still bears those emotional scars. My greatest regret is that I allowed her to remain in that toxic environment for five months. In an emotionally and physically abusive setting, five months might as well be five years. I placed my trust in the system instead of relying on my own ability to homeschool her. Although I was unsure how to balance a full-time career with the demands of homeschooling, I now see that I should have acted sooner. Academically advanced yet profoundly affected by trauma, my daughter became hypersensitive to every challenge. As her mother, I realized that if the public education system was failing her, it was up to me to find a solution.

I didn't have to wrestle long with the dilemma of balancing homeschooling and a full-time job because my body made the decision for me. The stress from my daughter's situation, combined with the demands of working over sixty hours a week as the Dean of Graduate Studies, led to a complete breakdown. I was diagnosed with chronic inflammatory demyelinating polyneuropathy (CIDP), a rare autoimmune disease, and my body failed to respond to intravenous immunoglobulin (IVIg) therapy. Everything in my life seemed to be signaling that a change was necessary. For the first time, I had no choice but to heed my body's warnings.

In my graduate studies, I had learned that due to its unregulated nature, homeschooling often resulted in academic setbacks when children returned to public schools. I was faced with the prospect of my academically gifted daughter being ill-prepared for college if homeschooled, or suffering further bullying if she returned to public school. Driven by the urgent need to protect her and provide a stable environment, I decided to take my chances in spite of everything that formal education had taught me about homeschooling. I was going to homeschool her through graduation.

4

The First Year

I was still learning how to navigate the adolescent mental health care system (or the lack thereof) with my daughter. She had severe anxiety in social settings, had begun cutting herself, and was diagnosed with everything from generalized anxiety disorder to schizoaffective disorder. Add into the mix that my son was entering the second grade in public school. I wish I could say my first year of homeschooling my daughter went smoothly.

I was emotionally spent and mentally exhausted. I needed a curriculum that would be easy on me as a parent, because the truth was that I didn't have the energy to think about it. I was on an emotional teeter-totter of saving my daughter's life and preparing her to live it as best she could. Every morning, I would hold my breath and listen for her footsteps on the stairs. Then I would exhale. On the mornings I didn't hear footsteps, I would have to will myself to climb the stairs. The physical act of doing so was agony as I tried to navigate the steps without losing my off-kilter balance, but the real mental torture of this morning ritual came with my uncertainty of whether I would find her dead or alive.

I think that's why I didn't resist my daughter's suggestion of using K12 as an academic option. K12 was a new online public charter school in Georgia that positioned itself as an accredited homeschool alternative.

I had neither the energy nor the mental fortitude to complete in-depth scholarly research. Soon, though, I realized that K12 really isn't homeschooling. It is simply public school online.

As I ventured into the realm of public online schooling, I soon found myself wincing every time someone confused it with homeschooling. It wasn't just a matter of semantics; the distinction ran deep. What bothered me most was the uphill battle of meeting all the requirements set by traditional public schools without the necessary support. Sure, they handed out curriculum packages, laptops gleaming with promise, and even lab supplies for those hands-on experiments. Yet despite these seemingly ample provisions, the reality was starkly different.

I was thrown into a world where the responsibility to make it all work fell squarely on my shoulders. The glossy brochures and introductory emails failed to mention the late-night searches for additional learning resources, the frantic calls to tech support when connections faltered, or the improvised kitchen-table science experiments in lieu of a proper lab setup.

In those moments, the true difference between being enrolled in a public online school and the autonomy of homeschooling became painfully clear. It wasn't just about where and when learning happened; it was about the level of self-reliance demanded when the school day extended beyond virtual bell schedules and into the uncharted territory of makeshift classrooms and parent-led lessons.

Among all the absent resources, the most critical one my daughter needed was access to a student success team. If she were to have one, I would have to build it myself. But it's hard building a team around a concept you didn't create using a curriculum you didn't select with the goal of meeting outcomes you aren't told about until you fail. Not to mention I also had the added responsibility of preparing her for the mandatory standardized test she had to pass to be promoted to ninth grade. That is the biggest difference between public online home- school programs and true parent-centered homeschool programs—in Georgia, privately homeschooled students are required to be tested only every three years. Moreover, the parent can select not only the test but also the testing method, a customization greatly needed to cater to the diverse learning abilities that prompted the need for homeschooling to begin with.

Academically, my daughter excelled, but emotionally, she was grappling with what her psychiatrist diagnosed as complex posttraumatic stress disorder (CPTSD). Witnessing her relentless effort was both heartening and heartbreaking. She would rise at 6:00 a.m. and often wouldn't rest until well past 1:00 a.m. Despite her unwavering dedication, she didn't pass the eighth-grade end-of-year test. This outcome solidified my decision to not send her back to public school; I couldn't bear the thought of her being held back due to a test she wasn't adequately prepared for in the first place.

The first year of homeschool was truly a year of transition. For me, it was all about unlearning everything my academic degrees ever taught me about how education should look and how learning actually happens. I was always taught that primary learning occurs in the classroom and only under the supervision of state-certified teachers who have both degrees and specialized academic credentials in the field that makes them an expert. Now I was forced to challenge this training and adopt the idea that learning occurs organically, a classroom isn't limited to a building, and that, as a parent, I knew more about the best learning style for my child than someone who had her on their class roster based on test scores and prior teacher comments.

What frustrated me the most about the K12 program was the amount of work parents were expected to do. The Georgia K12

Program (now GA CyberAcademy) used to require parents to function as the homeroom teacher. At first, their requests were simple, such as daily logins to the parent portal account, but then they started becoming more detailed—for example, parents had to log in before the student could do so. I was trying to navigate this online public charter school from home with my daughter while I was still teaching online college classes. Sometimes, I would be in the middle of grading assignments or discussions for my college students when I would get an alert that we were late for her login time. In the end, I reached my breaking point and simply handed over my login information to my daughter—I was beyond frustrated. This was not what I had anticipated when I enrolled her. The last straw came when K12 insisted she take remedial classes before they would allow her to retest. Throughout the year, I had repeatedly inquired about test preparation classes, knowing that in traditional public schools, students received such support before exams. It was infuriating to find that despite taking the same tests, my daughter wasn't offered the same preparatory resources.

By this point, I had thoroughly researched homeschooling in Georgia. I discovered that Georgia stands out as one of the most supportive states for homeschooling, granting families extensive freedom to craft their own educational paths without the need for accreditation. In fact, no organization in Georgia holds the authority to accredit homeschool programs.

The pivotal moment for me arrived when I submitted my Georgia Declaration of Intent to Homeschool to the Department of Education. This marked the beginning of my journey as an official homeschooling parent, empowering me with full control over our daily schedule and curriculum choices.

Choosing a homeschool curriculum differs significantly from selecting one for public school. In the public system, curriculum choices are typically made once a year for the upcoming academic term. As teachers, if we disagreed with the chosen curriculum, we had no choice but to make do and supplement it as best as possible. This was the approach I took during my initial year of homeschooling—a year marked by genuine disdain for the curriculum.

K12 offered a homeschooling option as well, albeit with mixed reviews. Despite its divisive reputation, it was the only familiar option available to me, so I decided to go with it.

In the end, my frustration stemmed from the extremes in some classes: either there was insufficient background information and examples to effectively teach a concept, or there was an overwhelming amount of information that made it nearly impossible to navigate to a clear understanding and solution.

So, there I was once again, just like in public school, with zero control over the curriculum I was expected to teach, spending my days constantly trying to supplement.

My daughter also grew disillusioned and frustrated with the K12 online homeschool program, as my constant supplementation meant she was essentially learning the same material twice. She said to me, "Mommy, when you teach it, I learn it, but when they teach it, it's just a waste of hours from my life that I will never get back."

My daughter had grown up watching me facilitate online classes and she often sat in my office with me as I hosted new faculty training webinars, where I trained new professors to teach online classes. Everything that went wrong in her online classes felt like a nightmare to her—like when they forgot to disable the chat feature during live lessons (students typing everywhere while the teacher tried to lead the slides), or when they locked everything down so tightly that she couldn't even signal for help during a live lecture if she needed it.

What really angered my daughter was that she was required to sit through that unorganized chaos. Finally, I told her to just log in to the live lecture and turn off the sound. Never once did it occur to me to drop the curriculum and make my supplemental material the entire curriculum. I wish someone would have told me at the beginning that it's okay to change up your homeschool curriculum—even if it's in the middle of the school year. If it's not working for your child, it's okay to replace it with something that will work better.

I overlooked significant flaws in my daughter's curriculum because my main priority was ensuring her well-being and recovery. Once that was stabilized, my attention shifted to finding the best academic curriculum for her. I grappled with evaluating and selecting curriculum, relying on the flawed "teach to the middle" approach.

***

Just as I figured out this chaos with my daughter, I found myself in yet another battle with the school system, this time for my son. It was at that moment the lightbulbs lit up, like the bright stage lights flashing on in a theater. I began to realize that the system for which I had spent my entire life advocating was flawed beyond my wildest comprehension. In fact, I was so consumed with my daughter's education that I almost missed the educational tsunami about to swallow my son.

My son spent kindergarten through fourth grade in public school. When each school year was about to begin, I always found myself praying to God, the universe, ascended masters, and archangels for divine intervention that he would get a good teacher.

His kindergarten teacher was a train wreck. Every school has that teacher—the one whom administration just keeps moving around from grade to grade in an attempt to help her find her sweet spot for success. In the case of this teacher, the school first moved her from grade to grade, then the county moved her from school to school. I guess it was an attempt for all of us to equally share in the misery of her inability to manage her classroom.

My son entered kindergarten excited to learn but was soon transformed into a reluctant learner. When I went on a school field trip with the class, I quickly figured out why. We were at the children's museum in Atlanta, and as the other classes were lining up to go to different exhibits, his class was out of control. They were running everywhere while the teacher stood in the middle of the museum lobby yelling. I was baffled that she did not know the most basic rule of classroom management: don't yell.

Moments later, my eyes locked with the teacher's eyes and we exchanged the teacher look—an expression educators share with each other, almost like a bat signal, to say, "Hey, are you okay? Do you need help?"

Normally when teachers exchange this look, a silent game plan is formed through nonverbal communication. With this teacher, I may as well have been an alien who had just landed on Earth, because she merely stared at me. I realized that not only did she have zero control of her class, but she also had no idea how to manage this situation.

I remember looking at my son and asking him, "Hey buddy, how does your teacher signal your class to line up for lunch or to walk silently in the hallway?"

He replied, "Mommy, she doesn't. Nobody listens to her. I do, but it's too loud sometimes and I can't hear."

A foundation-setting academic year was lost because he had a teacher with zero classroom management skills. I knew it would be an uphill battle to catch him up with all of the content he was missing. He was spending seven hours per day with her in a loud, chaotic, overstimulated classroom. No wonder he couldn't remember anything from class when he got home.

I remember when I asked the teacher for a Student Support Team referral for academics. She told me they didn't do this for kindergarteners. I later realized that *she* simply didn't want to do this, because she hadn't bothered to document her observations of my son in order to make him eligible for intervention. Most people don't know that even if you have a request from services from an outside provider, or even if you as a parent know that your child needs academic intervention or occupational services such as speech, the teacher must make the documentation for a referral.

It was actually my son's first-grade teacher, Mrs. Robin Berry, who pushed the process to help me get in-school speech services for him. I never told her so, but she reinforced my belief in humanity and educators. For the first time, my son felt capable of learning. It would still take an additional two years for the school to provide the services and by then, he was nearing the end of third grade. We had to cross so many tiers of intervention that by the time he did get the services, it was too late. Mrs. Berry was one step ahead of the system for her students in need, and she suggested adding small pull-out groups during one of our Student Success Team meetings. Mrs. Berry retired in 2017, and I will forever be grateful for her advocacy. I only wish there were more teachers like her.

I knew I had two options for my son—a 504 plan or an Individualized Education Plan (IEP). When I started advocating for an IEP, I was met with the response that an IEP and a 504 are essentially interchangeable. They are not. The IEP is crucial because it lays out the entire framework for a specialized educational journey, whereas the 504 plan focuses primarily on providing accommodations for accessing learning in school. A child cannot have both simultaneously, and often parents settle for a 504 plan without pursuing an IEP, which provides a more comprehensive and tailored approach to support their child's educational needs.

Not to mention that the IEP stays with students as they transition into higher education, whereas the 504 plan ends when they leave school.

My choice was clear. I began advocating for my son to get an IEP that would provide him with in-school speech services, modified assignments, extra academic support, and small pull-out group instruction. But this was not an overnight process. In fact, it took four years, with the help of a school counselor and his third-grade teacher, Dr. Alisha Wheeler, for the IEP to get approved. This resulted in my son beginning second grade without the support he needed.

I began to call this year of his schooling the "year of the beast," when he transitioned from loving learning to hating everything about it. What I didn't know at the time was that his teacher had forced him to stand in front of the class to read aloud knowing that my son struggled with both speech and reading. My son went silent after that year. The doctors called it "selective mutism"; I call it broken by a bad teacher.

In order for my son to keep up in public school, I hired Dr. Stacy Lawson, a veteran kindergarten teacher at the school, to tutor him two afternoons per week. I also paid out of pocket for speech services with an outside provider until the insurance benefits reached the maximum limit.

I finally saw the light at the end of the tunnel as he began third grade. His teacher, Dr. Alisha Wheeler, taught from the heart and turned her classroom into a community. As a result, the other students rallied beside my son and made him feel accepted, which was such a relief. By the end of the academic year, the school finally granted both an IEP and speech services (by now I had exhausted the lifetime speech service benefits through our private insurance policy).

When I started this journey for educational equality, I didn't know that I would become intimately acquainted with terms like sensory processing disorder, social anxiety disorder, selective mutism, written expression language disorder, significant speech language delay, and auditory processing disorder. I received three different diagnoses from three different child psychologists, who described my son as everything from "presenting with significant autism traits" to "exhibiting selective mutism." Even more frustrating was how they described me: "Mother is reluctant to accept diagnosis." I wasn't reluctant to accept the diagnosis—I just needed to know which one I was supposed to accept, because none of the observations and diagnoses supported the others. I had a school system trying to convince me that if my son would just try a little harder he could do it, and a team of professionals telling me that no matter how hard he tried he probably wouldn't do it. But what I needed most was to know how to navigate these uncharted waters, and that is what no one could tell me. No one knew how to guide me to manage the next step in the process.

When he was entering the fourth grade, I was very happy that he was set up with a great teacher—but this teacher ended up in an impossible situation. That year, she had twelve students with IEPs and one student with a behavior disorder. This wasn't a special education setting, just a regular fourth-grade classroom.

Nonetheless, the year was off to a great start. I thought my son's academic curse of good year/bad year rotation was broken. I celebrated too soon, though. When the teacher got sick and had to go on leave for surgery, a long-term substitute came in and told the entire class that she wasn't going to deal with twenty-three children reading twenty-three different books. She declared that the entire class was going to read the same book and promptly selected a sixth-grade-level novel, *Where the Red Fern Grows*. At the time, my son had a reading comprehension ability of 2.8, which equated to the end of the second grade. It was only at the start of fourth grade that he even attempted his first chapter book, *Bad Kitty for President*. When my son brought *Red Fern* home to me with the homework assignment—to read one chapter per night (no exceptions)—I knew in that moment that it was not going to go well between me and this teacher. The first night, we barely got through two pages of the first chapter. It was a hard book, but for a struggling reader, it was an impossible task.

I had to shift my focus from my daughter to my son. Since this was a long-term substitute teacher, I had to let her know that we needed to modify my son's assignments, but when I reached out to her, she shut me down. She was adamant that everyone was going to read the same book and complete the same homework assignment. I refused to break what remained of my son's spirit, so I became a fourth-grade student on his behalf. He would bring a page full of discussion questions home each night and I would do them after I put him to bed.

When we finally finished the book, I wrote her a note that said, "I have two PhDs—one in K-12 teaching and learning and one in criminal justice. Now I can proudly say I completed the fourth grade twice and the second time around, I read a sixth-grade-level book." I sent that email to every administrator at the school and the grade level chair. Within two weeks the substitute was gone, but that wasn't good enough of a solution. I had enough. If the public education system was going to fail my son, I was not going to be am party to the crime.

I was absolutely terrified at the thought of homeschooling a child with a lot of special needs learning labels—especially my own son! I can empathize with parents who are scared of pulling their special needs children out of what they think is an educational safety net. However, after watching all of the educational milestones we gained during his third-grade year slowly fade away, I had no choice.

The morning I told my son I was going to homeschool him, we were in the car on the way to school. As we pulled out of the driveway, I looked into the rearview mirror and said to him, "I made a decision last night about your school. We do a lot of things in our house, but one thing we don't do is support insanity or insane people. Your teacher is out sick, your school has lost its mind, and the inmates are running the insane asylum. If we are all going to go crazy, I need to be the one in control of it."

My son stared at me blankly from the back seat.

I tried again. "What I'm trying to say is, you know how I homeschool your sister?"

He nodded.

"Well, I'm going to homeschool you too."

Then came the smile, and as my announcement really sunk in, he jumped up and down in the seat. "I'm going to be HOMESCHOOLED!!!" he screamed. "Mommy, thank you! You're the best teacher ever!"

And I took him to school that morning for the first time in a long time with a smile.

5

Homeschool Not Aloneschool

In addition to homeschooling an academically gifted high school student coping with complex PTSD from bullying, I also had an academically delayed elementary school student. I found myself embracing the role of a homeschool mom to two special needs learners. With my daughter, we went through four different high school curricula—K12, Connections Academy, and several stand-alone sets before we ultimately settled on a self-paced curriculum combination of LifePac Homeschool Curriculum and dual enrollment classes at Georgia Piedmont Technical College. My daughter and I became a team, making it a habit to review the curriculum together. She was engaged in and committed to her own learning journey. I took this win and finally exhaled. I had been doubting myself since we started this journey, but this win made me feel like I finally got it right.

My son was different. He was at least two or more grade levels behind, so I really struggled with where to start. I thought that, unlike my daughter, he couldn't engage with me at any meaningful level about the curriculum. I was wrong. I just didn't know how to present it to him in a manner that allowed him the opportunity to engage in his own learning process. The first year, we tried Time4Learning. That was a good start for helping us transition into homeschooling, but midway through the year, he got bored with the repetitive structure.

I found myself stuck; there was a part of me that wanted to give up but I couldn't, as doing so would have meant ultimately giving up on my child. Their father was no support through this—in fact, we were in the middle of a divorce and he was using my decision to homeschool in his argument for custody. He even filed for an emergency court hearing to get a court order and open a Department of Family and Children Services (DFACS) case against me for educational neglect. If I gave up, I would be allowing him and the system to win. I feared I'd be sending a message to my son that I was only going to fight when it was easy and that I would only fight so far. I needed my son to know that I was just as committed to fighting for him as I had been to fighting for his sister.

I couldn't think outside of the box but I had to be willing to explode the box. I was homeschooling a child who had struggled in a traditional learning environment. I was going to have to pivot on a dime, and this wasn't even the hard part. For all practical purposes, I was going to have to lay the path while walking on it.

This is the point when many new homeschool parents hit a wall and consider throwing in the towel. But for me, this was the exact moment I realized I needed to think beyond conventional methods and completely rethink our approach. Homeschooling a child who hasn't thrived in traditional schools requires constant adaptation. No one handed me a step-by-step guide for homeschooling because in reality, there isn't one. Each home is unique, and every homeschooling journey toward the same goal takes its own route.

When I tried to ignite my son's interest in reading, I turned to

Real Kids, Real Adventures. I figured it would be perfect for him since the stories were based on real-life TV episodes. Unfortunately, the books turned out to be too advanced and he was still struggling. What I later realized was that even though the books were great for us to read together, he really wanted to read them alone, yet he didn't have the reading fluency or comprehension skills in order to feel successful doing so. He got frustrated and I felt like I was failing, so I decided to take it back to the basics. I went to our local teacher supply store and bought him workbooks for second and third grade. I tore off the covers, three-hole-punched the pages, and put them into a binder.

I told him, "I just need you to try so that I can know where you need help." Success! He finished five pages without ever asking me for assistance because I had found his true level.

If you notice that your child is struggling in a subject area, don't be afraid to stop, assess the situation, and determine why your child is struggling. I hate to hear people say, "My child is just lazy." I always respond, "No, your child isn't lazy. You and your child just have different work patterns and learning styles. You haven't taken the time to understand your child's learning style because you were too busy forcing your child to fit into a perception of a two-hundred-year-old academic mold." Lazy is just a byproduct. You have to get to the root cause of the problem.

I still remember that first morning I gave my son my makeshift language arts binder. Before he even opened it, he said, "I can't do this. I'm not good at language arts." Many people would see his reaction as "lazy" or "uncooperative," but I understood the root cause of his anxiety. He simply lacked confidence because he had been learning in the confines of a broken academic model that wasn't designed for him to succeed in the first place.

Homeschooling authentically gave me the level of flexibility to meet my child's true needs. I had to step away from trying to force my child to work on the curriculum for his public school grade level and allow him the freedom to work on the curriculum that matched his ability level. We would eventually get to his grade level but I knew I had to build his ability level confidence first.

The next year, my son was going into middle school and I knew we were still behind academically, so I decided I needed to build my own well-rounded student support team. I turned again to Dr. Grogg and asked her for recommendations.

Dr. Grogg suggested that I look at the Orton Gillingham approach and contact Devorah Lowenstein with Atlanta Educational Associates. I had studied Orton Gillingham in graduate school and was familiar with it as the first teaching approach that was designed specifically for struggling readers. It breaks reading and spelling down into the smaller-skill units of letters and sounds. I had been reviewing the Orton Gillingham approach for struggling readers for two years (and I'd even bought some books on how to apply it), but I had no real desire to thoroughly learn the approach and then implement it with my son.

I wanted an expert who had already mastered this approach and could help retrain my son's reading strategies. So, I hired Devorah to help my son improve not only his reading strategies but also his reading confidence and writing abilities. When I first mentioned to my son that we were going to bring in a reading tutor to help him, he was reluctant, to say the least. Our first conversation started out with him reminding me of everything he couldn't do. "I don't know why you want me to work with a reading tutor. I had a reading tutor in public school too, but I just can't remember what I read."

I had to remind him over and over that this was homeschool, not public school—and not public school at home, but homeschool. In this school, he was going to remember what he read because we were going to put some new tools in his reading tool belt. I explained it like this: "Remember when you were building that toolbox in the garage with your scout pack?" He nodded.

I continued, "What if the only tool that I'd given you to build the toolbox was nails, no hammer. Could you have built the toolbox?"

He stared at me. By now I had learned that his silent stare didn't mean he didn't understand the question. It meant that he was searching through his mental file cabinet (as we called it) for the answer. He finally replied, "I would have to have a hammer and nails."

I saw this as my moment to build a learning connection. "You're right. You would need both a hammer and nails. So, when you were in the public school, they gave everyone nails and some kids learned how to make a toolbox with only nails. But other kids needed both the hammer and the nails to build the toolbox. I want you to work with a new tutor who has not only a hammer and nails but a drill, screws, and wood glue as well, so that you can seal up the edges. Her name is Mrs. Devorah, and she wants to meet you. She wants to work with you so that you can not only read better, but so that you will be able to understand what you are reading. Let's just give her a chance for thirty Tuesdays."

I had learned with my son that everything had to have a definitive start and end. Thirty Tuesdays was something he could mark on the calendar. He never actually acquiesced to this new approach, but then, he never refused either. I knew if I truly wanted to engage him that I would treat this like a military-style mission. My son loved all things war-related, so I told him that we were going to have to do some trench work every Tuesday.

"Trench Work Tuesdays" started in August 2015 as I drove him almost an hour from Conyers, Georgia to North Druid Hills, Georgia to meet with Devorah. It wasn't easy. I was still a single parent. I was finalizing my divorce and I still had my own chronic degenerative health condition; nevertheless, I had to show up for my children as their mom, their advocate, and their primary educator. Trench Work Tuesdays were hard for me and on me. Some days I just wanted out of the trench, but I couldn't show my son how hard it was, or else he would see that as permission to slack off and slow down.

It took three years, but when he finished working with Mrs. Devorah, he was finally reading on grade level, as well as writing four-page research essays and citing his sources. I fought so hard for the IEP when my son was in traditional schooling, yet the irony isn't lost on me. For none of these accomplishments would have been possible if I had listened only to the advice of the IEP team at his elementary school, who wanted to convince me that celebrating his ability to read fifty sight words was the maximum goal. No matter how hard they tried to reason with me, there was something deeply flawed in that rationale that honestly didn't sit right with me, first as an educator and second as the mother of a young Black son—a Black son who will be alone in this world one day because I know that I am not immortal. There will come a day when I won't be here to advocate for him, and there is no way that I am going to leave a whole Black man in this world with the ability to read only fifty sight words.

My son and I were still attending Wednesday morning classes at the Atlanta Homeschool Cooperative when I realized that he seemed very comfortable with a fellow homeschool mom named Leanna Ampola. I knew that Leanna was a Montessori-trained educator and that she was launching her own program called Growth Montessori. I also had heard that she used manipulatives to teach math concepts. I asked if she would be willing to work with my son. I told her that he was several years behind in math and that I had spent the last two years focusing on improving his reading fluency.

When my son started working with Leanna, he couldn't memorize multiplication facts. It took him years to memorize his address and phone number. His brain isn't wired for memorization, and the ability to recite math from memory is a century-old, public-school model. I asked Leanna whether she would be comfortable using a visual-based math curriculum, and she was overjoyed because that was her teaching style. We selected MathUSee and I administered the placement test so that we could determine where to begin. My son started at the Gamma level and within two years, he had completed the Zeta level! A child who started out with no knowledge of how to multiply numbers had relatively quickly mastered multiplying fractions and percentages. His confidence in his academic abilities was soaring, and over time I could see that he was no longer a reluctant learner but a ready learner.

My son created a wonderful relationship with his tutors, and I now had the foundation for Team Trench work. Some people raise their eyebrows when I tell them that I hire reading and math tutors for my son. The reality is, in Georgia it is legal for a homeschool parent to hire a tutor to provide academic instruction. This means that even if you homeschool, you don't have to do alone school. You can hire tutors for those academic subjects that you either aren't comfortable teaching or simply don't want to teach. To maximize my son's academic ability, it was a better choice for me to function in a support role by hiring subject matter experts in the two fields and to have them teach him the concepts.

What I learned on this journey with my son is that you can't just think outside the box. You have to think beyond the box and even build your own box. You have to be willing to design your own curricula with your own team, and you have to be confident in what you are doing in order to silence those who don't understand the path you are on.

I was so busy building bridges to educational access for my children that I didn't even realize I was actually creating the foundation of a transtheoretical model of behavior change homeschool program.

6

Homeschooling With an IEP

If I can say anything to a parent who is thinking of homeschooling, it is this: Be prepared to experience resistance. That resistance will make you question your own decision-making, and it will make you feel underprepared for taking charge of your child's academic journey. As soon as I shared with my son's IEP team my decision to home school him, I was met with resistance—first from the IEP committee at the school and later from my ex-husband. Several members on the committee said things like, "You are going to cut off his access to services that he needs," or, "You are reacting from a place of frustration. You just need a cooling-off period." His father tried to convince me that homeschooled children were isolated and that the only way our son was going to get socialization was by attending public school.

But the best plea was, "His teacher has an endorsement as a reading specialist."

To that one I replied, "Yes, his teacher on paper does have an endorsement … but that teacher is sick and the last long-term substitute you gave me was two french fries short of a happy meal. I will take my chances."

I was determined that if my child was going to be on a sinking ship, then at least I would be the captain.

I didn't realize when I started this journey that in order for me to stand my ground, I would have to do it alone. The lack of support made it difficult at times to resist questioning myself and my efforts. It even escalated when one of the well-meaning IEP committee members made a call to our local Department of Family and Child Services (DFACS) to report me for educational neglect. This was my second DFACS report for the same issue, and I was ready to fight. I had a three-ring binder that contained all of my college transcripts, my university teaching classroom observations from my Dean of Academic Affairs, and educational learning plans from outside experts I had hired to show that by homeschooling, I was providing a better support system for my son than the public school system could. I had also joined the Georgia Homeschool Education Association (GHEA) and the Homeschool Legal Defense Association (HSLDA). No, I wasn't going to fold. They wanted to fight; I was ready to do battle. That single action sparked a fire within me—a fire that ignited my journey to revolutionize my children's educational well-being. It soon became a movement, spreading like wildfire beyond the boundaries of my own family.

The first thing I did after leaving that IEP meeting was try to join every single special needs homeschool group in Georgia I could find. I was desperately seeking a community for support and solidarity. But in 2013, there weren't any such groups for me to join. So instead, I joined every single non-religious homeschool Facebook group, which quickly became overwhelming. Some groups were so structured that they felt like traditional school, while others felt like organized chaos at best.

I tapped into these homeschool groups to gain immediate insights, but what I craved most was reassurance that I was on the right path. Ironically, despite my PhD in K-12 teaching and learning and my role in developing courses for public school teachers, I found myself questioning whether I was making the best choices for my son. My situation was unique; unlike most homeschoolers I met, who had only ever homeschooled, I was navigating the transition from public school to homeschooling.

I had all of the academic credentials but I was missing the homeschool confidence. My feelings left me wondering how many other parents wanted (or needed) an alternative learning option, but felt incapable, forcing the path of the traditional education system. This realization became my call to action.

Somehow, one of my never-ending rabbit hole searches led me to the Atlanta Homeschool Cooperative (AHC). I immediately became a member and as soon as I got access to their Facebook page and group, I knew I had found my tribe. The biggest difference about AHC was that a lot of the homeschool moms in the group were professionals—educators, lawyers, doctors, and artists who were both homeschooling and working. Homeschooling for them was a life choice, not a full lifestyle. Other homeschool groups I had tried to join in the past always made me feel like I had to have a full homeschool lifestyle, which simply didn't fit our family.

I still hadn't found a curriculum, but the support I got from AHC gave me the courage to build my own. The first year I homeschooled my son, we completed a lot of workbooks. I found myself having to sit with him often to do these; above all, I didn't want him to get as frustrated with homeschooling as he had become with public school. We tried out Time4Learning, a highly ranked online homeschool curriculum. It had a student-centric learning approach and I thought it would be a good stopgap measure until I could create a better game plan.

However, my son struggled with the learning format because he felt it kept repeating the content. I later realized it was grade-level focused and very reading-intensive, while he still wasn't reading on grade level. I decided the next best step was to get my son tested so I could truly know where he stood academically, but I didn't trust a lot of professionals anymore. It was through AHC that I found a colleague from my elementary teaching days. Dr. Kathryn Grogg was now a homeschool mom, and she offered academic testing through her company, Grogg Educational Consulting, LLC. I trusted Dr. Grogg because I knew that even with my son's separation anxiety (which I later realized caused him to score low), she would take the time to distinguish between what was true anxiety and what was a lack of knowledge. I knew that I was going to have to build my own support team for my son, and Dr. Grogg was my million-dollar team captain. Dr. Grogg tested him, and although he was a fifth-, soon to be sixth-grader, he tested at a high third-grade level in reading and a low second-grade level in math.

I will always be grateful to her for what she did next—after we looked through the results together, she turned the paper over and said, "Let's make our plan to get him on track." I felt a rush of validation and inclusion unlike anything I had experienced before in a professional setting. No one had ever used that pronoun with me in this context. The others were quick to give me handouts with intervention strategies, but no one had ever proposed including me in "our" plan. It was a profound moment of feeling seen and valued. For the first time since I had started our homeschool journey, I didn't feel like I was having to do everything alone. I was building a team.

***

As soon as the plan began to form for my son, my daughter slipped into a mental spiral down another dark hole. This is the part of parenting a child with a mental illness that I never heard anyone talk about. One moment, everything is good, all of the plans are on track, and there is a light at the end of the tunnel. The next moment, it feels like that light is actually the headlights of an oncoming train with no warning horn.

She was entering the tenth grade and I knew she was bored with the new high school curriculum. I remember begging her adolescent medical team to please do an attention deficit disorder (ADD) screening because I knew from my own research that ADD/ADHD presented differently in girls than in boys. They dismissed me and stuck with their original diagnosis of schizoaffective disorder. Once again, I was on the train track alone, trying anything I could think of to get her refocused. It was at this point that I suggested to my daughter the idea of becoming a dual enrollment student. I knew she would research it IF I presented the idea to her at the right time and IF she felt like she had enough control over making the final decision. Those are a lot of big IFs for a parent who is homeschooling because an IF could become a NO in seconds, and I was honestly growing tired of always having to have a backup plan for the backup plan.

She was so excited about the opportunity to take some of the dual enrollment classes that she researched class descriptions and professors for months. I was beyond excited to have her get out of the house, and looking forward to having a few moments to exhale. Parenting a child with a mental illness is like constantly holding your breath, waiting for the next shoe to drop—or fly. I've become adept at bobbing and weaving to avoid the impact, but it is exhausting.

I learned about the dual enrollment option for homeschool high school students during a workshop at the annual homeschool conference. I remember sitting there thinking this will be a game changer for us—I can finally get my daughter engaged with other learners who are at her academic learning level, which will allow me an opportunity to focus more on my son. I thought we were doing better because she was so excited about dual enrollment at first, but then her attitude shifted completely and I wasn't sure why. Only later would I learn that she had been told that dual enrollment students couldn't take online classes. It was the anxiety of returning to the classroom that was causing her latest mental health crisis.

Homeschooling for me was both a choice and an entire lifestyle change. I had to first shift my mindset about what I thought education was versus what I had been taught that education was. Next, I had to shed all of those preconceived ideas that had been ingrained in me from my own education experiences. None of those ideas was going to be able to sustain me because I was entering into uncharted territory. I have grown to believe that learning doesn't only occur between the hours of 8:00 a.m. and 3:00 p.m. Monday through Friday in a classroom with walls—true learning is a lifelong process. I understood that by becoming a homeschool family, I was making a commitment to nurturing that process, no matter how it appears to others.

My daughter was experiencing dual enrollment anxiety because of what happened the last time I tried to send her to a classroom. A local private school heard about her being a victim of bullying and offered her a scholarship on network television. I thought it was a bad idea to do this on TV, but if I turned down the offer with everyone watching, then I would look like an ungrateful parent who was in crisis and refused to accept help. That whole experience just created more trauma.

Now, my daughter was afraid of failing me because the private school that had offered her the scholarship ended up kicking her out; her anxiety and trauma were too much for them. I will always remember the morning I got the call from the school that said, "Come pick her up. Never bring her back. This isn't working for us." What I realized that morning was something about private schools I had forgotten—they function like private clubs that can revoke your membership at any time. Then it's up to you to figure out what to do. I was angry. I was hurt. I was disappointed. But for everything I felt, I knew that my daughter's feelings were amplified because she always internalized everything. She was going to feel like she had failed me instead of realizing that yet another system created by adults had failed her.

After I worked through the dual enrollment anxiety attack with my daughter, I was seriously questioning whether I had made the right choice, but I knew for her sake I had to stay the course. She needed to see that, even at the height of an anxiety attack, she not only had the skill set she needed to succeed but the mindset as well. I found myself giving my daughter the tough-love speech I had given thousands of times at graduate student orientations: "Graduate degrees aren't awarded to the smartest students—they are awarded to the most determined. This is a game of chess. With every move you make, you have to keep the endgame in mind. I don't expect you to walk in here with all of the answers, but I do expect you to bring me your best attempt to find the answers. None of this is easy but I promise you, the tassel is worth the hassle."

We sat there in silence for a while, with only our breath filling the space between us.

"Mommy, I'm scared to do this. I'm scared to try. What if I fail?"

My heart sank. I took her hand in mine and said, "I saw your future, and guess what? You didn't fail. You succeeded."

We both laughed and she said, "When did you become psychic?" "I don't have to be psychic to know my daughter. I'm your number-one fan and I know you aren't going to fail."

As we were nearing the end of my homeschooling journey with my daughter, I realized at some point she was going to have to graduate— but what would that look like? As I searched for answers, I found myself down many rabbit holes with a lot of data points that weren't connecting. All I had wanted to create for my children was access to an education in an optimal learning environment that maximized their learning styles. But I also knew that at some point all of this had to end, and I had to find some way to document everything I had done. I needed a school name to put on the homeschool records. That's when I had the idea—use the name of the Facebook group Tiers Free Homeschool Cooperative and make it Tiers Free Academy, so that the cooperative was the curriculum and the academy was the documentation. I remember feeling a little like a mad scientist in a lab as I sat with the idea. It sounded so simple that there had to be a flaw in the plan. Could it really be this easy and, if it was, then why wasn't everyone doing it?

I googled "Homeschool Diploma Print Companies," and the results left me in absolute awe. Not only was this legal, but there were also entire business operations that printed diplomas for homeschool families. My idea wasn't so crazy—people were doing it and apparently had been for years. It's just that no one talked about it.

When I finally issued my daughter a homeschool high school diploma and watched her get accepted into two D1 universities, I let out a deep exhale of both celebration and validation.

7

The Tiers Free Model

A few weeks after my daughter's graduation, I was sitting with my neighbor Crystal on the back deck with a glass of wine. Our daughters were close in age, so I was caught off guard when Crystal's youngest daughter Beth shared with me that the bullying at the high school had been too much for her, and that she had dropped out during the end of her eleventh-grade year. Just hearing that she gave up one year away from graduation was a sucker punch to my gut. I struggled to swallow the lump in my throat.

I asked Beth if she would be open to getting her GED if I would help her study. These words rolling off my tongue, almost uncontrollably, shocked me; I'd struggled so much with homeschooling my own children that I had never thought of tutoring anyone else. Beth gladly accepted my offer of help, so I went home that night and began an internet search that would ultimately change my life.

Later that evening, I happened upon a site called Do Something. Org, and I couldn't believe the statistic blaring across the front page. Every twenty-six seconds, seven thousand students drop out of high school in the United States. I wondered how impacted Georgia was by these numbers. My search continued.

In 2013, according to the Georgia Budget and Policy Institute, 865,704 Georgians aged eighteen through sixty-four did not have a high school diploma or a GED. I couldn't let this continue without trying to be a part of the change. My research intensified over the next several weeks. I found that in 2011, a study from the GED Testing Service found that within six years of earning a GED, about 40 percent of GED recipients enroll in college—but most drop out within a year. Only about 1 percent earn a bachelor's degree.

I was confident that I could help Beth study for the GED because I taught GED classes through a grant at a literacy center when I was in graduate school. While I knew that these data points were old, I still felt inspired.

But then I realized, if 865,704 Georgians are without high school diplomas, the system isn't working and won't fix itself. It was up to me to change the system. I was determined that not only would I make sure my children didn't become a statistic, but I would also not allow any child in my community to become one either.

I was determined that Beth was going to have the same feeling of being a high school graduate as my daughter, and that her mom was going to experience the same validation and celebration as I had. I was going to do this even if no one from the academic community was willing to support me. The truth was, by now I had gotten a reputation in academic circles for fighting against everything. But I was fighting only against broken things. That didn't matter, though, because anyone who was trying to remain in good standing with their university began to stay far away from me.

While it hurt, I honestly didn't care anymore. They could sit in their ivory towers and pretend there wasn't a crisis, but I couldn't because I didn't have tower access anymore. I was on the ground and there was work to be done. If I didn't use my knowledge that the system was broken and consequently, I allowed Crystal's daughter to become a statistic, then I would fail. I was not going to be that person.

As I delved deeper into homeschooling and homeschool high school diplomas, I realized how the traditional adult education system often prioritizes profit over genuine educational needs. Here's why: Many parents assume education ends at eighteen and after that, anyone who hasn't completed traditional schooling must navigate adult literacy programs. Few bother to read their state's homeschooling laws because homeschooling isn't typically on their radar. However, homeschooling offers unique freedoms. You can continue educating your child past eighteen and award them a homeschool high school diploma whenever you deem appropriate. Why? Because your child remains your responsibility regardless of age, and as a homeschooling parent, you have the autonomy to shape their education. Some parents tailor their curriculum towards trade certifications like plumbing, electrical work, or multimedia production. This flexibility is the essence of homeschooling: empowering parents to chart their child's educational journey. What I didn't know at the time was that the GED as I knew it no longer existed. It was no longer owned by a nonprofit organization and it was no longer a workplace-focused GED. Now, it was owned by a for-profit company called Pearson and was redesigned in 2014 to be a Common Core-focused GED.

Common Core initially promised a unified educational standard across the United States, ensuring consistency in grade-level materials from state to state. While the concept seemed straightforward and beneficial, its execution tells a different story—a classic case of theory losing its way in practice.

After the GED was revamped to align with Common Core standards, only 20 percent of test takers managed to pass all five sections on their first attempt. With my background, I understood the significance: a staggering 80 percent of test takers failed one or more sections. Historically, those who failed were unlikely to return for a retest.

I remember thinking that this would be so much easier if high schools used the same strategy that colleges did—allowing students who had dropped out to return. But unlike colleges, high schools operate like those exit-only lanes on the freeway.

Until 2014, thirty-two states allowed students to drop out of school at the age of sixteen, but no one was capturing the data on dropouts until these students turned eighteen. I realized that those two years were an educational sweet spot. If only I could somehow reach the students after they dropped out and provide them with an alternative path to a diploma! This became my mission.

During my extensive research on the GED, I explored every available resource related to it. Along the way, I stumbled upon an internet search regarding employability after obtaining a GED, leading me to a forum where recent GED graduates shared their struggles and experiences in finding employment. It was there that I discovered some significant limitations: GED holders faced challenges in pursuing certain nationally-based jobs and were ineligible to join the military without additional requirements.

Unlike before, employment applications no longer simply asked if applicants had a high school diploma or GED; they now specifically inquired if the individual was a high school graduate. For GED recipients, answering truthfully often meant automatic disqualification. I found this infuriating.

Even more surprising was the military's updated stance: they no longer accepted GED graduates directly. Instead, those with a GED who wished to enlist were required to complete at least one semester of college courses. Considering the time it takes to enroll in and complete these classes—approximately one year—the delay could potentially diminish the individual's interest in pursuing a military career.

The sum of all these parts was sobering. Once a student dropped out of high school, the path to recovery and finding success became increasingly grim.

I couldn't set Crystal's daughter up for a life of limited opportunities and closed doors. A homeschool high school diploma would be a better solution than a GED, and I knew how to issue one since I had just done so for my daughter. My mind was spinning. Then it hit me—even though Beth had dropped out of school, there wasn't an age limit for homeschooling; as long as the diploma is issued by the parent, it is legal.

That's when I sprang into action.

8

The First Graduation

My educator light bulb was turning on. Instead of trying to make Beth fit into a system I already knew was broken, why not build a system for her that would give her a real opportunity. When a student stops attending college, none of her work disappears. College dropouts don't have to start over or enter remedial programs; they simply pick up with their classes where they stopped. Why couldn't I do the same thing for Beth? I had everything I needed in the homeschool cooperative.

My brain was going so fast that I was struggling to keep up in my own thought process. I had to call Crystal because even if I could figure all of this out, if she wasn't on board, I couldn't implement the idea. I didn't even look at the time when I called.

"Doc? Is everything okay?" No one in Crystal's family ever called me by my first name. I had been Doc ever since I graduated with my first doctoral degree. That's when I looked at the clock. It was almost midnight.

"Everything is fine. I'm so sorry to call so late but I've been on the phone all day and I had an idea to help Beth get a high school diploma but my idea can't work if you don't want to do it. I can call back tomorrow."

The tone of her voice changed immediately. "A high school diploma? How?"

When Crystal tells the story, she says that I was talking faster than a rat running up a drainpipe. I just remember being so excited that the words were falling all over the place and I felt like I had to get everything out at once. "I've been down a rabbit hole of Georgia homeschool law and I've even talked with a lawyer from the Homeschool Legal Defense Association. In Georgia, it is legal for a parent to issue their own homeschool high school diploma to their child at any age. I know how we can get your daughter a high school diploma. How soon can you get me her high school transcript?" We both sat there on our phones in silence.

Finally, Crystal spoke. "So I need to get you a copy of her transcript. Tell me where I need to go to do that and I will go as soon as they open in the morning. My daughter is going to have a chance to graduate. Doc, thank you."

And that's how the Tiers Free academic intake process began. The good news was, once I got Beth's academic transcript from her high school, I saw that she needed only four classes.

She was excited about the possibility of obtaining her high school diploma and now I had to make it happen—even if it meant I would have to build a curriculum myself. And that was exactly what I did. I used different curriculum vendors for each subject and Beth had to give me her work every Friday.

Over the next four months, we diligently followed my newly crafted curriculum every day. Each time Beth completed a class, I felt a mix of joy and sadness. I was happy for her progress, yet acutely aware of the many others in similar situations who also needed this chance. I was driven to extend this help because the staggering statistic of nearly 866,000 Georgians without a high school diploma still weighed heavily on my mind.

I was struggling with how to package my ideas when my friend Terrance, suggested I name my organization The Dr. Annise Mabry Foundation, Inc. and use Tiers Free Homeschool Cooperative (Tiers Free Academy) as a program under the foundation. Five months later, Crystal and I were planning the first graduation ceremony. We decided to have it in August—right before her daughter's birthday. The excitement in both our homes was contagious. The moment the graduation package with Beth's diploma arrived was surreal. We held the box for the longest time before opening it. I couldn't stop staring at the box because what we had done was still sinking in. When I looked up and saw Crystal's face, I was speechless. She was crying those silent tears that only a mom who has fought the fight understands. Mrs. Becky Wood, Crystal's mother, suggested that I needed to use my "doctor gown" to present her granddaughter's diploma. Mrs. Becky loved celebrating my doctoral degree, and every time we were in earshot of anyone who would listen, she would announce proudly, "This is Dr. Mabry but we call her Doc." She always insisted that I take my robe to the cleaners because it needed to be pressed.

A week before the living room graduation ceremony, my robe went to the cleaners for its official pressing. I never told Mrs. Becky that when I graduated with my doctoral degree, my parents weren't able to make the flight to see me have my degree conferred, so having her celebrate me this way felt nice. I vowed that as I continued on and gained more graduates, I would ensure they had someone in the audience to cheer when their name was called. I know how loud that silence sounds when you walk that stage alone. Graduations are celebrations and celebrations have people present.

As we all assembled into the living room for our graduation ceremony, I gave my neighbor's husband my phone and asked him to play the graduation march. Since he was a DJ, the song played over a very large speaker; immediately I felt myself being transported back to all of the graduate school ceremonies at the university. But this time was different. This time, the graduation song sounded powerful, while I felt like I was standing on a cliff about to freefall into something so exciting and transformative beyond my wildest dreams.

I marched with my graduate behind me into the living room full of her family. I conferred her high school diploma and we did the traditional tassel turn. Mrs. Becky was laughing, clapping, and screaming as if we were in a huge auditorium. She later shared that she had never had an opportunity to graduate or watch her own daughter graduate, so this moment felt almost unreal for her.

Later that evening as the family celebrated, I found Mrs. Becky on the front porch. In our Southern culture, there is something special about front porch conversations. I pulled up a chair and when I started to sit down, Mrs. Becky immediately jumped up.

"DOC! Don't sit on the gown. I'm getting a hanger so we don't mess it up with these chairs. I didn't wipe them down."

I laughed and assured her that the chairs wouldn't mess up the gown, but I also knew that me telling her and her actually listening were two different things. So, I acquiesced. We sat there, just the two of us with my gown hanging on the porch. She kept rubbing the velvet. "Doc, we gone have us a whole houseful of high school graduates," she said with pride, in a way that felt more like a suggestion than a statement. She leaned in closer to me and although her eyes were still full of excitement, her face was now sad. "I never got to graduate and her mom never got to graduate. You know this is the first child she has got to see get a high school diploma. I hope you can get her other daughter graduated too."

I had to address the elephant that she had brought onto the porch. I reached over to touch her hand and asked, "Mrs. Becky, are you telling me that neither you nor your daughter or your entire family have high school diplomas?"

"Doc, I got pregnant in school and I wasn't allowed to finish. Well, they might have allowed me to finish but the way I saw it was I had a baby and I needed to take care of my baby but I always wanted to know what it felt like—to wear that gown and have a tassel. I always wanted to see my name on my diploma and I wanted my daughter to get her diploma."

That night, I made three promises to Mrs. Becky—one, that she would see her name on a high school diploma; two, that she would see her daughter graduate; and three, that I was going to give her a whole house full of high school graduates.

At the university level, we gave honorary degrees to celebrities and community icons often, so I decided to do the same thing for senior citizens at the high school level. In May 2017, Mrs. Becky Wood became my first honorary high school graduate. In April 2018, just two years after she watched her granddaughter graduate and almost one year to the day that she graduated, Mrs. Becky Wood had a stroke and was moved to hospice. Crystal, her daughter, and Scottie, her daughter's husband, were scheduled to graduate the following month. Three days after Mrs. Becky was moved to hospice, Crystal left me a voice message.

"Doc, Mom had a rough night. All of the grandchildren came earlier. She is in so much pain but she's holding on for something. We thought it was the grandchildren but she's still fighting."

I knew what she was holding on for and I knew what I had to do. There was no time to press the gown. I grabbed it out of my coat closet and called Crystal.

"I know this is going to sound crazy but we do crazy, right? I made a promise to your mom that she would see you graduate. She's holding on to see you graduate. I'm on my way. Please tell her that the graduation ceremony is starting in an hour."

The hospice was a good half an hour drive from my house but I made it there in twenty minutes. I had my robe, my neighbor's robe, and her diploma. I'm sure I looked like a hot mess graduation express but I had a front porch promise to keep.

As I was opening the door of the hospice room, I played the graduation march song. I remember hugging Crystal and then setting the phone on the bed. I reached for Mrs. Becky's hand and held it the way we always did, interlacing our fingers. I leaned over the bed and whispered, "Mrs. Becky, I'm here. We are going to have a graduation ceremony today. I promised you that you would see your daughter graduate and I'm here to deliver on that promise." That afternoon, I graduated her daughter.

On the drive home, "Broken Halos" played on the radio and I found myself in quiet contemplation, deeply moved by the profound and magical event that had taken place. Later that night, Mrs. Becky passed away peacefully.

I walked out onto my back deck and stared into the darkness. My neighborhood was silent but my thoughts were screaming. I held my stomach like there was a baby growing inside of me and I rocked back and forth in deep thought as tears fell down my cheeks. Mrs. Becky's death pained me greatly, but in the middle of my deep sadness, she was talking to me. I could hear her. She had become my doula and we were about to give birth to my ultimate purpose right there on my back deck in the still of the night. Her dying wish was now my battle cry. It was time. I was going to give her that whole house of high school graduates. And all I wanted to do was call and tell Mrs. Becky this, but I couldn't.

9

Trauma-Informed Academic Program

My dad was my entire support system. When he died in 2017, it was Mrs. Becky who reached out to me each day. After her death, I felt like the last remaining leg of my broken three-legged stool was gone and I was on the floor. I knew I had to get up again but I honestly didn't know how. When someone called me to help them get their high school diploma, I got up and in autopilot mode, got to work, since I learned a long time ago that grief is a passage not a place and that I had to make friends with time. I thought I was pushing through the passage but in reality, I was actually pushing down the emotions.

I was dealing with my own personal grief journey while still trying to help my daughter navigate her classroom trauma. Even though she was a high school graduate and was still working with a counselor for complex post-traumatic stress disorder (CPTSD), she experienced crippling anxiety when she had to do anything remotely connected to a classroom environment.

I remembered what I thought at the time was her irrational reaction to not being allowed to take dual enrollment classes online. I will be the first to admit that I didn't know nearly enough about trauma when I was dealing with my daughter, but I wanted to learn more because I was her support system. I found myself down another research rabbit hole in the middle of the night. It was the first time I read the words traumatic grief. Losing Mrs. Becky suddenly had created traumatic grief in me and the more I sat with it, the more I saw the parallels between grief and trauma. I was able to identify how these experiences impacted not only a student's life but also their ability to learn.

I decided that Tiers Free program was going to be a trauma informed program in both policy and practice. I became intentional as I created a trauma-informed homeschool cooperative that focused on building an inclusive, supportive community and prioritizing the emotional well-being and academic success of all students. I intentionally selected contractors and nonprofit partners who understood trauma and its impact on learning and behavior.

As I started to look at online curriculum vendors, I specifically looked for those who had integrated social-emotional learning (SEL) into the curriculum. This is important because it helps students build resilience, self-regulation, and coping skills. I wanted my homeschool cooperative to encourage positive, trusting relationships while fostering a culture of respect, empathy, and mutual support.

I knew from working with my neighbor's daughter that I needed to use a strengths-based approach that recognizes and builds on each student's unique abilities and interests. I also wanted to implement restorative practices to address conflicts and behavioral issues in a constructive manner, emphasizing empathy and understanding over punishment.

Trauma-Informed Academic Program

This early trauma-informed foundation is still deeply interwoven into our operational fabric. We continue to engage families and the wider community in the cooperative's activities and decision-making processes to create a strong network of support. We also continuously assess and refine the cooperative's practices based on feedback from program graduates, ensuring that the program remains responsive to the evolving needs of the students.

10

The Movement

It all started with a moment on a porch and a need to help my neighbor with tools I had used to help my own children. Since that first graduation in the living room in 2016, one thousand families have used the program to issue their own homeschool diplomas. Our oldest graduate was seventy years old and our youngest graduate was sixteen. Currently, the homeschool cooperative has over three thousand families enrolled as members and accepts student referrals from three rural school districts. We are also the only homeschool cooperative to have multi-year contracts as an educational services provider with two county jails. The graduation ceremonies are now so large that they are often standing room only in some of the largest local venues that often seat up to five hundred.

When I started this journey in 2012, it was to save my own children. I never dreamed this would become something that would ultimately save entire families with children.

I would often remember Mrs. Becky and how she would correct me when I called the program Tiers Free Homeschool Cooperative. If she was in earshot, she would yell, "It's Tiers Free Academy because you are making school possible for students who couldn't go or didn't go to school."

I always resisted, but as the program began to grow in the community, the name that stuck was Tiers Free Academy. Mrs. Becky got her wish. In the communities where we have a strong presence, we are known as Tiers Free Academy. I then have to remind program participants that Tiers Free Academy operates under the Tiers Free Homeschool Cooperative.

One thing I learned early in my homeschool journey was that curriculum is an expensive investment. This factor often made the decision to homeschool unobtainable for many families. Since I had made the homeschool cooperative a program under the foundation, this made it eligible to receive grant funding. I used the funding to purchase curriculum in bulk and then provided it free of charge to families in need. Our grants were small, which limited the number of families we could subsidize. The word about our assistance was spreading like wildfire, while our waitlist was growing faster than our funding. I dreamed of the day that I could immediately help anyone who enlisted our services.

The pandemic compounded my challenges significantly. COVID-19 altered the educational landscape for all, and its impact on students persists. Within the academic community, much discussion surrounds the learning setbacks caused by COVID-19. While I acknowledge these losses, I also contend that the pandemic exposed pre-existing, often overlooked learning deficiencies. This further fueled my mission. In 2021, I was invited to apply for grant funding from the United Way of Greater Atlanta to become a Learning Loss Service Provider for seventy-eight rural, persistent poverty counties in Georgia. This invitation was historic, as United Way contracts typically went to organizations deeply integrated within school districts, often providing traditional afterschool tutoring or other support for at-risk students. Being designated as a Learning Loss Service Provider by United Way allowed us, for the first time, to accept every student who had been on our waiting list. As a result, we witnessed a threefold increase in our graduation numbers.

2023 was a monumental year for us as we were the first homeschool cooperative in Georgia to host a high school graduation ceremony at Albany State University, a 121 year old HBCU in rural Southwest Georgia. The auditorium where we hosted the ceremony was packed. I remember standing on the stage and looking into the audience with tears in my eyes. For those families and the graduates, this was a moment they never thought they would have. For me, it was a moment when I could look back in shock and admiration for how far I had come. To add to my astonishment, that same year, I also hosted eight graduation ceremonies in eight different graduation venues in seven different counties.

Since awarding Becky Wood with an honorary diploma in 2017, we have now awarded over ten honorary high school diplomas. These may just be my favorite, as they never fail to transform a family.

As if 2023 couldn't have been a more exciting year, The Tiers Free Homeschool Cooperative was the only homeschool cooperative in Georgia to receive a Proclamation of Service from Georgia House of Representatives District 93 incumbent, Doreen Carter. It was also the first to host a graduation ceremony at Albany State University. In June 2024, Georgia Senator Jon Ossoff sent personal letters of congratulations to each Rural Communities Diploma Program graduate. This recognition at the state and federal levels is typically reserved for elite public and private school graduates. The fact that our graduates are now receiving this same level of recognition is unprecedented and underscores the value we bring to the community.

Our Rockdale County Class of 2024 had 114 graduates and

by December 31, 2024, we will have issued our one thousandth homeschool high school diploma. From graduating one student in my neighbor's living room in 2016 to graduating almost one thousand students less than a decade later is powerful.

Today, with over two thousand families, we are the largest online grant-funded homeschool cooperative in Georgia, offering diagnostic online reading and math assessments as well as a full academic curriculum for grades K-12. The graduation ceremonies are supported by local businesses and local government officials, while retired NFL players serve on our graduation committee.

Community development was the founding vision of the Dr. Annise Mabry Foundation, and community service remains a key tenet. We tell our families that Tiers Free Homeschool Cooperative is a working community program. The program works because the community works the program.

I'll never forget one graduate who returned to help at our outdoor booth in the middle of a storm. When I insisted that I would be okay on my own, my former student looked at me and said, "When everyone else gave up on me and didn't think I would graduate, you didn't leave me. I'm not leaving you." And we put on our rain ponchos and sat under the tent together.

Every day I wake up knowing that every twenty-six seconds another student drops out of school in America. Honestly, I don't think there is anything we can do to stop dropouts, because their reasons for doing so aren't always academic.

The majority of my students are under the age of nineteen, and while their reasons for dropping out are different, the end result is always the same—they made a life-altering decision, and without the Tiers Free Academy program, they wouldn't have had a second chance. When I share my story at education conferences, people always want to know how my children are doing now. My oldest is twenty-five and although she graduated from college, she still struggles to maintain consistent work. The trauma she endured in school from being bullied has become a ghost that haunts her. Some days her social anxiety takes over and she gets overwhelmed.

We talk about her journey often and she says to me, "Mommy, the one thing that kept me from being a statistic was you. When I watched you fighting for me and I knew how sick you were, I knew I had to keep fighting too." This was the wind beneath my wings that I didn't know I needed. I will always believe the best lessons in life aren't the ones you teach your child but the ones your child learns by watching how you navigate the storms and disappointments in life. I think the biggest thing that has kept her on track is her consistent mental health team, who has finally found the right medication for her.

My son is now twenty and is finishing his first year in college. He is studying aviation mechanics and recently got an A in college physics. A child who the Individual Education Planning (IEP) team told me would never read more than fifty sight words is living on campus and just got an A in college physics.

Neither of my children would have made these achievements had I simply accepted what I was being told would be their future. I will always remember sitting around the huge conference table when I told the IEP team that I was going to withdraw my son to homeschool him. My hands were trembling but I sat firm in my conviction. I stood firm on my declaration that if my family's ship was going down, then I was going to be the captain. No one else was going to sink the ship but me. And I somehow found my voice in that meeting. I learned how to become an educational advocate not because I was trained to advocate but because my children's lives depended on me advocating for them. Fighting for my children cost me what I thought was my dream career in academia, but it was in fighting for them that I stoked a new fire inside of me. I used to say that I was homeschooling by necessity because I had no other options. Today, I am grateful for the lessons that homeschooling taught me. Without those lessons, I would have never gotten the inside knowledge I needed to guide other parents like me through the maze of fragmented systems and broken bridges. Only those who have walked this fire can understand how to navigate the flame.

This homeschool cooperative program is my gift back to my community. In school, I was always the obedient student. I always colored in the lines and stayed in the safe zone. As an educator, I have always been called disobedient because when I know something is wrong, I won't back down until it is fixed or at least acknowledged. I tell the parents who reach out to me for help that sometimes they have to be disobedient when they have tried to work within the system without success.

I always know the parents who aren't ready to find their voice to fight because their reply starts with, "Thank you, but the school said it is better to…" I've learned to simply say to these parents, "You're welcome, and I'm here if you need to come back."

11

Macon County Chiefs' Diploma Program

In 2018, I met with a newspaper reporter in Oglethorpe, Georgia. Her name was Mrs. Roger Ann Davis and she was covering an information session meeting I was holding at the Oglethorpe Police Department regarding the Macon County Chiefs' Diploma Program. But before I tell you about Mrs. Roger Ann, I first have to tell you about Chief Rachael Lee Hart.

The City of Oglethorpe had just made history by appointing their first female police chief. This was a bold progressive move in a predominantly conservative small town. I was excited to meet Chief Hart, as her reputation preceded her. In her first ninety days, she fired half of her department and the municipal court judge. She had one simple directive to her officers: If you are coming into my city to only write citations, this is not the agency for you. This was a bold directive from a female police chief in a male-dominated field, especially in a rural community where law enforcement agencies were struggling to fill shifts. We spoke on the phone a few times about my foundation and what a partnership between us might look like.

I had just received my first corporate grant of $20,000 to create an innovative community program that would impact workforce development. The city and the mayor for whom I had originally written the grant bailed on me. This was my first grant, so I definitely didn't want to give the money back to the funder. I had to find another municipality with similar demographics of race, adults without diplomas, and a high crime rate.

I found all three of these in Macon County, Georgia in the city of Oglethorpe. Thirty eight percent of 18-24-year-olds didn't have a high school diploma and 46 percent of 24-34-year-olds didn't have a high school diploma. The city's crime rate was 69 percent; five known national street gangs were operating within 2.1 square miles, and there was one street that officers simply didn't patrol because it was gang territory.

I knew that if we could somehow get high school diplomas into the hands of residents, the community would change. My dad always told me that the most dangerous person in the fight wasn't the one with the most skills but the one who had lost hope. I was about to use the same Georgia homeschool law that saved my children to bring hope to a small rural community.

The next call I made was to Chief Hart.

"Chief Hart, I want you to understand that nothing like this has ever been done before, but if we can pull off this pilot program together I think we can transform your community. Can I come down to your office and present it to you?" I asked. I also shared with her the statistics that I found. The day I arrived happened to be the state court probation day.

"Dr. Mabry, it's not that I don't trust your data but I need to collect my own," Chief Hart said in her leather American flag cowboy boots and hair in a ponytail hanging out of a baseball cap. She got a clipboard and a pen, then stood at the door of her police department asking the people reporting for probation whether they had a high school diploma. Nine out of ten people on state probation in 2018 didn't have a diploma. It was one thing to see the data on my computer, but it was hitting me differently when I looked into the eyes of the people who were the data.

That afternoon, we sat in Chief Hart's office for the longest time in silence before she said, "Come ride with me." We got into her patrol car. "Dr. Mabry, I pray to God that this program you want to do is the real thing," she said as we pulled up to the first house. There were children in the yard. "We have folks like you from Atlanta who come here all the time with all these fancy programs and they pull out as fast as they pull in. But me, well I can't pull out because I coached these kids and some of their parents at the recreation department. I grew up here and I'm going to protect these people here. Your program sounds good—almost too good, and if you aren't going to stay for the long haul, go ahead and leave now before you hurt them. They've been hurt enough."

I didn't know what to say, which is an abnormality for me. I sat there in her patrol car as we drove all over her city.

When we returned to the police department, I said, "Chief, I'm not going to hurt them. I promise you that. I'm not just someone from Atlanta. I grew up about thirty minutes away from here and I graduated from Sumter County High School in 1992. If I see for one moment that I am hurting them, you won't even have to ask me to leave. I will leave on my own."

"Wait. You went to Sumter County?" the Chief inquired. "I did. I was the class of 1992."

"I graduated from Sumter County in 1994," she said with a wide grin. Sumter County was a small school and I definitely didn't remember anyone named Rachael Hart. I did, however, remember a great softball player, but I couldn't remember her last name. There was no way this was the same person.

We were both struggling to remember each other. We began

naming mutual friends and finally, I had to ask whether she'd had a different name in school. She told me Hart was her married name. Twenty-six years later, life brought us full circle and I knew that my program was going to be successful because there was an unspoken oath among Sumter County graduates—you aren't just classmates, you're family. You look out for your family. You take care of your family. You protect your family. You show up for your family.

We got out of the patrol car and walked back into her office. "Dr. Mabry, tell me your idea again and let's figure out how to make this work. You've got my full support."

To effectively partner with law enforcement in implementing a diploma program, I understood the crucial need to bridge the gap between police officers and civilians. Drawing from my prior experience, I recognized that addressing this divide required a specialized program, ongoing training, and diligent oversight. As I reflected on my journey, it felt like a full circle moment, aligning my past experiences with my current mission. I felt not only challenged, but also excited that my cooperative would be expanding into areas I had never imagined.

There were three parts of my newly designed program—education, engagement, and outreach. Education for the officers meant changing department operations from the inside out and using more proactive policing than reactive. It also meant that officers had to learn the individuals they were serving rather than simply responding to a call. They had to identify the root cause of the issue that created the call in the first place. Engagement was deeply rooted in the public's ability to trust that the officer responding to them genuinely wanted to help, and the officers' ability to trust that the community they were serving genuinely wanted their help. Outreach meant creating high visibility, low-engagement activities beyond traditional community policing activities such as passing out stickers and candy. Our outreach program involved creating a corporate partnership with

Walmart for weekly donation pickups of all of their clearance items and creating a community outreach closet that officers could access for families in crisis. The items from this community outreach closet also provided toys and school supplies for two new programs: Christmas with a Cop and Backpack with a Cop.

The following week, Chief Hart asked me to come to the city council meeting, where we both presented the full program and not only asked for their vote of approval, but also for office space for my foundation inside the police department. The council vote was a unanimous yes. I had not only created the Southwest Georgia Community Policing Resource Center but also the Macon County Chiefs' Diploma Pilot Program.

Chief Hart began promoting the Chiefs' Diploma Program on the department Facebook page, and she asked the other two police chiefs to share her post. However, her request fell on deaf ears. I was disappointed but not defeated. They simply didn't know who I was, I reasoned. Chief Hart wasn't defeated either.

"Dr. Mabry, we will keep inviting them. They will come around. It just takes time," she explained.

We decided to hold an information session on a Saturday morning in November. The morning of the orientation it was pouring rain, and as Chief Hart and I sat inside an empty meeting room with a table full of food, the minutes ticked away. Finally I got up to start cleaning. "What are you doing? You giving up on us just like that?" Chief Hart asked.

"Chief, no one but you even cares that I am here and what I'm trying to do. Thank you for trying to help me. I appreciate you."

"Well, just hold on, Miss Atlanta, give me an hour. There were some people interested. Let me go to their houses and see if they need a ride getting here. Can you just wait before you pack up? Plus, it's raining and you know ya'll Atlanta folks can't drive in the rain," she teased as she walked out the door.

While she was gone, I sat down with my lead volunteer, who had been reluctant to bring this program into South Georgia. She wanted to keep the program and the operations in the Metro Atlanta area. Right about now, I was inclined to agree with her.

The first person to walk into the meeting when the rain slowed was Mrs. Roger Ann Davis, a news reporter from *The Citizen Georgian* paper in Montezuma, Georgia. I soon learned that Mrs. Roger Ann had been a member of the Macon County Board of Education and she was deeply interested in this diploma program, as well as curious about how it differed from the GED. As I waited on potential participants to arrive, I explained to Mrs. Roger Ann why the program is so effective, going through every step of the process. I then explained that in order to qualify, students would have to provide a high school transcript, and that any class in which they received a 60 percent or higher would be considered passing. They would take only the classes they needed to take and if they had work experience or certifications, those would count as elective classes.

Mrs. Roger Ann said, "Dr. Mabry, this sounds wonderful, but what do you have in place to ensure that your program graduates can't cheat in the classes and that they can actually read when they finish the program?"

I explained how the online classes used a test bank that randomized test questions and answer selection order so even if two students got the same question, they wouldn't have the same answers to choose from. I also told her that all graduates would have to write a 1,200- word capstone essay that described their journey to becoming a high school graduate. I was midsentence when I heard the door open, and in walked a soaking wet Chief Hart with one of her council members and four potential students.

"Dr. Mabry, meet your students. They are here to learn more about the program, and they want to get their high school diploma," Chief Hart explained. In a room I expected to remain empty, my pilot program gained the slightest of traction, giving us the momentum we needed to keep pushing forward.

Our first graduation ceremony was held at the elementary school cafeteria where twelve students received their diplomas. Standing next to one of our graduates was her grandmother, beaming with pride as she received an honorary diploma. The energy in the air was contagious, and the effectiveness of the pilot program began to spread, creating a whole new arena for the Tiers Free Homeschool Cooperative to be impactful.

Epilogue

Educational Disobedience isn't about being defiant; it is about surviving. Reflecting on this journey, I am filled with a sense of accomplishment and gratitude. The path was neither straight nor easy, but it was necessary. My story, like so many others, is a testament to the power of persistence, courage, and love. I think one of my proudest moments was when I got a message from a class of 2023 graduate to let me know she'd gotten accepted into Princeton. Then, in the same day, another graduate from 2022 sent a message to say she'd received her Associate Degree as a Pharmacy Technician. Since starting this program, I have had graduates get accepted into GA Tech, UGA, University of Arizona, and Albany State University, just to name a few.

On June 1, 2024, after I finished two of my largest graduation ceremonies, I resigned from the day-to-day operations at the foundation. During that final month, I graduated 253 students with only an administrative team of three people. As I am writing this chapter, I am sitting at the kitchen table of a two-bedroom apartment in Civitavecchia, Italy. I live every day with a sense of tremendous gratitude, not only for having had an opportunity to homeschool both of my children, but for having taught other parents to follow in my steps. Looking back, I see the moments of doubt, the tears, and the sleepless nights. There were times when I questioned my decisions, when the weight of responsibility felt overwhelming. But I also see the smiles, the breakthroughs, and the incredible growth of my children. They have shown me that with the right support and environment, they can thrive beyond any limitations imposed by traditional systems. These moments of success, no matter how small, reinforced the importance of our journey.

One of the most profound lessons I've learned is the value of resilience. Education is not a one-size-fits-all model, and when we face challenges, it is crucial to adapt and persevere. This journey has taught me to be flexible, to listen to my children's needs, and to trust in our ability to find solutions together. It's about embracing the process of learning, both for them and for myself.

Educational Disobedience has also shown me the importance of community. I could not have done this alone. The support of other parents, educators, and advocates has been invaluable. Sharing experiences, resources, and encouragement has created a network of like-minded individuals dedicated to transforming education. This community has been a source of strength and inspiration, proving that collective effort can lead to significant change.

The concept of Educational Disobedience extends beyond homeschooling. It is about questioning the status quo in all educational settings. Whether you are a parent, teacher, or student, you have the power to advocate for a more individualized approach to learning. This might mean pushing for changes in public schools, seeking alternative education models, or simply being more involved in your child's education. The key is to remain proactive and engaged, always looking for ways to improve and innovate.

My children's successes are not just their own; they are a testament to what is possible when we refuse to accept mediocrity. They have thrived because they were given the freedom to explore their interests, learn at their own pace, and develop a love for knowledge. This is the essence of true education. It is not about memorizing facts or passing tests, but about fostering a lifelong passion for learning.

I hope this book has inspired you to question, to challenge, and to seek out what is best for your own children or students. Remember, true education goes beyond the confines of a classroom. It is a lifelong journey that should nurture curiosity, resilience, and a love for learning. Each child deserves an education that speaks to their unique potential and empowers them to achieve their dreams.

As we move forward, let us continue to push the boundaries of what education can be. Let us create spaces where every child can succeed, regardless of their background or abilities. This means advocating for policies that support diverse learning needs, investing in teacher training, and ensuring that every student has access to the resources they need. It also means being willing to innovate, to try new approaches, and to learn from our failures.

Let us never forget that our actions today will shape the future of tomorrow. The work we do now to reform education will have a lasting impact on generations to come. It is a responsibility that we must take seriously, and it is a challenge that we must rise to meet. By embracing Educational Disobedience, we are not just changing the way we educate; we are changing the world.

Thank you for joining me on this journey. Your interest and support are crucial to the success of this movement. May you find the courage to embark on your own path of Educational Disobedience and make a lasting impact on the lives of those you teach and love. Together, we can create a system that truly serves all students, one that values individuality, fosters creativity, and prepares our children for a future full of possibilities.

In the end, Educational Disobedience is about more than just education. It is about advocacy, equity, and the belief that every child deserves the chance to succeed. It is about breaking down barriers and building a better future for all. Let us commit to this vision and work tirelessly to make it a reality.

It is my dream that those who come after me will continue to follow the model I created and ensure that what happened to 866,000 Georgians without a high school diploma never happens again.

Maybe that's why I am drawn to rural, persistent poverty communities that have low literacy rates and high numbers of working-age adults without high school diplomas. I often tell everyone that I am my ancestors' wildest dreams; for my grandfather, I know this has to be true.

Appendix A
In Their Own Words

I kept my promise to Mrs. Roger Ann Davis about ensuring that the program graduates could read and write. For seven years, Mrs. Roger Ann covered every single graduation ceremony for us in Macon County. She always made our story front page and we were always above the fold. Since that first class of thirteen graduates, over three hundred students have graduated. Chief Rachael Lee Hart retired in 2021 and accepted a position with the foundation, first as the program registrar, then as the official program manager of Community Outreach and Engagement in 2024. The Macon County Chiefs' Diploma Pilot Program officially ended in 2021 and was renamed the Rural Communities Diploma Program. Chief Patricia Barber, who was appointed to the Marshallville Police Department in 2019 and retired in 2023, accepted the full-time position as the Director of Intake and Assessment for the Rural Communities Diploma Program. I also made the capstone writing assignment a mandatory graduation requirement for all program graduates. The capstone essays you are about to read were written by program graduates over the last decade. Some will make you laugh. Some will make you cry. Some will make you question everything you thought you knew about programs and educational practices that were supposed to be safeguards and pathways but instead were giant, gaping sinkholes.

My capstone editorial review team consists of Sarah and

Nimra. These two women read and edit every single essay we receive. Nimra has the additional task of working with graduates to transform their essays into motivational speeches that are shared at the graduation ceremony.

These are their words and their stories.

Emmett's Story

I'm my mother's oldest child and the forgotten part to my mom's story. The part you'll often hear my mom talk about is how she was the dean of one of the largest for-profit universities in the country. You hear about her experience but you never hear about the children and the families who had to watch our family member who was often the breadwinner and usually a very significant parent be traumatized in the process of all this.

Yes, she made it, but at what cost to her and to us as her children? When I have tried to speak my truth and tell my side of the story, I've often been shut down and told to not tell my business or my family's business or things like that.

I have watched as the suicide rates for Black women in academia are rising, and I'm not being quiet about it anymore. What I grew up with was two emotionally unavailable parents because you can't be emotionally available and traumatized at the same time. It's literally not possible.

My brother and I grew up emotionally neglected. There. I said it. People who knew my parents would cringe when I tried to say this as a child. The reality was there was a lot of neglect on the inside, and while it may have looked like we had it all on the outside, it was the inside where everything was crumbling and nothing was there.

My mom was our primary caregiver, and her career in academia often superseded our emotional needs as children. On the outside, my mom was able to hire a nanny and a team of caregivers but what we needed the most was a caring parent. Like I said earlier, you can't be emotionally available and traumatized at the same time. I despise academia to this day because what it stole from me I will never get back. My childhood was stolen. Memories that I could have made with my mom are nonexistent—even when she took us on vacations, she wasn't present in the moment because she was too afraid to disconnect from the university.

I have decided to share all of this now because Black women are dying as a result of toxic academic culture. I am sharing all of this because it is my healing too, and my mom said Educational Disobedience was about all of the ways that the traditional education system is broken. Well, you can't just talk about how a system is broken without taking an honest look at the human impact of that broken system.

Our reality growing up was that there wasn't a family system or structure of support or anything like that. What people have to understand is that when a parent is taken away from their household, this doesn't always mean they are physically taken away. When a parent is emotionally taken away from the home, the parent is effectively removed and that causes the entire family structure to crumble, and naturally that is very traumatic to the children who have had to pick up the pieces.

If there's one thing I want to make abundantly clear about this very specific part of telling my truth is that there was nothing more insulting than regularly being told by others that I should be grateful for experiences that were destroying me. I was always told that I should be grateful for all the things I had and I knew that these things were literally eroding my upbringing, my family structure, and all the systems of support because the reality for Black children is that if you do not provide them the support within the family and within the home they're not going to get it as an adult. They're going to have to go out and find it or pay for it but it's not going to just be given to them and that's the reality.

Essentially, people expected us to be happy. I felt like they were telling us all, "Look guys, you should be happy that they're spraying a poisonous spray and yes, we understand that it's going to kill some of you but the more you are sprayed, the more resilient you will become. You want to be resilient, right?"

My reality was I didn't care about being resilient. My reality is I suffered with a lot of internalized emotions for years. I finally realized that it's part of the system.

It's part of the game because what better way to destroy your family than to get you happy and excited about things that are inevitably going to lead to your own self-destruction. That is my part of the story and I don't want to talk about my truth until we're ready to talk about that.

My mom developed cancer twice in that toxic academic culture. I actually remember my mom during one chemo session being so sick but the university was still forcing her to finish certain tasks before they would approve her FMLA. I had watched my mom do her job long enough that when she fell asleep, I took her login and passwords and I finished her work for her so that she could rest. There are some that will say what I did was wrong, but what was wrong was the university not allowing my mom the opportunity to rest and to heal the way that she needed to when she was sick.

I have firsthand lived experience being told that I should be happy about the destruction of my family and losing my parents. Some say that it's hard when you lose a parent because they've passed away but you don't really understand grief until you've had to grieve somebody who is still living. People who have never had that experience will never understand what it feels like daily to have to look at your parents in the house with you but they are not emotionally available for you. That's a next level grief that you don't understand until you've been through it. My mom wanted her lasting legacy in academia to be how she disrupted the educational system that broke us. But I think what she forgot is a system that wasn't designed for us to succeed in the first place can't break us.

2019 Brandilyn Cromer "Thrive with Pride"

My struggles with traditional schooling started when I came out as bisexual. I was going to school in a small town and people in traditional schooling weren't very accepting of my sexual orientation and yes, I got bullied—a lot.

But it wasn't the bullying that made me quit school. It was when a girl who I had been dating accused me of raping her because her grandmother found out that she was attracted to women. Her grandmother didn't approve of same-sex relationships. That girl didn't want to risk ruining her relationship with her grandmother, so she ruined my reputation at school instead.

So not only was I being bullied for being bisexual, I also acquired the reputation of being that girl who forced herself onto other girls. It is no surprise then that I was extremely isolated.

Thank goodness I still had sports. Sports was my lifeline and kept me grounded. But then I got injured and had to have knee surgery. While I was out of school recovering from knee surgery, the rumors started again and now the only outlet that I had in playing sports was gone. I was overwhelmed. I was tired of fighting the rumors so I just quit school.

It was a decision that weighed heavily on my entire family—especially my mom and my grandfather.

When I learned about the Macon County Chiefs' Diploma Program from Chief Hart's post on Facebook, I called her to see if the program was legit and she said yes. Orientation for the program was on a cold, rainy Saturday morning and honestly all I wanted to do was sleep. Chief Hart called and said she was coming to pick me up to make sure that I didn't miss signing up.

Accepting that ride from Chief Hart changed my life. This program actually gave me a chance to receive my high school diploma rather than my GED. When I learned that this program had the support of the Atlanta Pride Committee, I realized that I could apply to receive a Thrive with Pride Scholarship here. It was the first time that I discovered that scholarship money existed for something besides sports.

I was even more excited when I found out that I had been selected as the first rural Georgia Thrive with Pride Scholarship recipient. Receiving the Thrive with Pride Scholarship really showed me that people actually cared about me and that an entire community of people who I never met loved me. The Thrive with Pride Scholarship gave me the boost I needed to finish the program.

My advice to others would be to go through this program, get your diploma and move forward with your life. Since I've received my diploma, I'm working on finishing my Certified Nursing Assistant (CNA) license, then I'll be going back for my Licensed Practical Nurse (LPN) and hopefully bridge over to a Registered Nurse (RN). Life has been great since I've received my diploma.

2020 Jessica Stephens "My High School Journey"

Wow! My journey through school has been a very different experience. Let me explain that a little more, so you all will have a better understanding.

When I was in elementary school, I remember I would get in trouble every single week for either talking too much or not paying attention. When I was in fourth grade, my mother took me to the doctor for a checkup because she believed I had hearing problems. She said I talked very loud all the time. Imagine that. I ended up getting my adenoids taken out and when I went to school the following year, my behavior was still bad but my grades improved!

The truth is when I went to school, I was just releasing the frustrations that I was experiencing at home. At home, I was being sexually abused. I was placed into foster care when I was in the sixth grade but when we went to court and everything was finalized, I was sent back home.

My behavior was really bad in school and I got expelled during both my sixth and seventh grade years. My eighth grade year, I was homeschooled online but I never attended because I didn't have any drive to do my school work. I was on an ankle monitor and probation at this point. I ended up informing my probation officer of the abuse and she took me out of the home that day. I was placed back into foster care. I was sent to a residential program in Bowdon, Georgia (Carroll County) called KidsPeace. I completed my eighth grade year there. The staff and the teachers I had there really made me feel like I was part of a family, so everything improved with me. My behavior, my grades—everything about me changed.

I decided that I wanted to live with my dad at the beginning of my ninth grade year, so I transitioned into my dad's home. But I hadn't ever dealt with the trauma I had endured as a kid so I started acting out again. I started skipping school and making very poor choices. I ended up stealing the janitor's phone at school and got caught.

The trouble I was causing my dad and grandmother was just too much to endure at the time, so I was back on the road to go to another residential treatment facility. My tenth grade year started at Anne Elizabeth Shepherd Home for girls in Columbus, Georgia. Again I started to feel like I was part of a family and grew strong bonds with the staff there. They all gave me that mother feeling and sensitivity that I was longing for. I went to school on the campus and I was making almost all straight As. When I would go to my cottage dorm area at night, the only thing that made me happy was learning. So I studied every single night. It was so fun to me and gave me hope in my life. In the middle of my tenth grade year, I graduated parts of the program and I was able to attend public school. I went to Northside High School in Columbus, Georgia but due to some issues of confidentiality and treatment, I was pulled from school and started my eleventh grade year back at Anne Elizabeth Shepherd Home. A few months later they ended up placing me back in the public school.

Keep in mind that as I was bouncing around from school district to school district, my high school credits were being lost. I was retaking classes that I finished or not being placed into classes that I needed because each school had their own registration system and none of the systems were connected. All of these credit transfers created a big mess.

So I ended up skipping school and making poor choices once again. The Home did an emergency transfer for me to go to another group home. So in the middle of my eleventh grade year, I was now at a group home called Arabella in Waverly Hall, Georgia.

Arabella was very small and only had about ten girls living there. It was different for me because I was used to homes with one hundred or more girls. I was still continuing to make straight As and Bs the whole eleventh grade year. A year later I was transitioning out into a foster home. This lady was my CASA worker through the Department of Family and Children Services (DFACS). So I did the beginning of my twelfth grade year at Centennial High School in Roswell, Georgia but she kicked me out of her house at 7:00 a.m. on my eighteenth birthday.

I went to my dad's house for a few weeks while DFACS was trying to find me somewhere to go. Since now I was eighteen, placement was very limited for me. I ended up getting my own apartment through an Independent Living Program (ILP) through DFACS. I was still in my senior year when I got transferred to Alonzo A. Crim Open Campus High School in Atlanta. My credits were so messed up and I was in a credit recovery program. Thus, even though my GPA was above 3.5, I would not be allowed to graduate as a valedictorian.

This was the first time that I had all online classes and that made things very difficult. I ended up dropping out with two credits left. I was basically kicked out of DFACS and lost my apartment.

I was homeless with no high school diploma so I jumped into the streets and never had any time to go back to school. School was always kind of a thought in the back of my mind but it didn't matter anymore to me.

I got arrested a few times and had babies back to back. My last time in jail, I was informed of a program that could greatly improve my life. I met Kasey McClure, went in the 4Sarah program and was reunited with my kids. I was given an opportunity to go back to school at the age of twenty-two.

4Sarah helped me to get enrolled in the Tiers Free Academy Program. I was enrolled in the online classes through Dr. Mabry. At first it was a bit difficult so I asked Dr. Mabry for help. When I talked to Dr. Mabry for the first time, I was so amazed. She believed in me more than I believed in myself. She believed that I was going to finish the program and that I would graduate with my high school diploma. I remember feeling amazed that she talked to me for a whole hour!

For the first time in a long time, I started to dream about my future and not my life in the present. I was telling her I wanted to be in law enforcement and—wow—to my surprise, this woman instantly started to help me carve out my roadmap for exactly that future. A few weeks after that talk with Dr. Mabry, I started to do the schoolwork that was required. I stayed up all night doing my schoolwork. I would wake up to my baby girls and then go to work. I was tired but I stuck with it every day and finally I completed my classes!!!! I remember the feeling I had and I just looked at my baby girls sleeping in their beds and I cried.

I was so happy. I finally did it! Now I am looking for colleges and I really am happy that I know that a career choice for me is not impossible!

For the first time in a long time, I have hope. Now that's something I have never had even when I was a child.

2020 Katiesha Tiera Smith

I learned about the Macon County Chiefs' Diploma Program on social media. At first, I didn't believe the program was real until I saw it firsthand. As I watched the class of 2019 graduate and then get accepted into colleges, I wanted to get my diploma too. I was so excited! I called Dr. Mabry and asked her to sign me up.

I struggled in the traditional education system not because I couldn't do the work but because I wasn't focused and didn't want to do the work. I had teachers that cared about me but they didn't know how to connect with me or how to motivate me. Then my grandmother got sick so I was only going to take a few days off to help my mom take care of her. A few days became a week and a week became a month. Then I had missed too many days so I just dropped out of school.

I started attending the South GA Technical College GED classes after I dropped out of high school. I took the GED test and failed it so many times that I just gave up. Honestly, I thought the Chiefs'

Diploma Program was going to be just like the GED program but it wasn't. I tried to quit the Chiefs' Diploma Program so many times but Dr. Mabry wouldn't let me. I remember once when I had fallen behind in my class because my mom had gotten sick and I was giving up. Dr. Mabry sent an officer from the police department to ask me what time I was going to be logging into my class for the day. When I explained that I was going to take a break because my mom was sick, Dr. Mabry said, "I'm sorry to hear that but when are you going to finish your work?"

I learned a lot more that day than just what was in the class. This program forever changed not only my life but my family's life too.

Dr. Mabry was firm and tough. She tells all of us: "The only thing I give you is thirty days to complete a class. You are going to earn every letter on your diploma that says High School Graduate." I remember the day that I finished my last class. I had finally earned my high school diploma. I hadn't even logged off the computer yet and Dr. Mabry sent me the application link for South GA Technical College. She said there were no breaks in education from this day forward. And she's right. Next year, I am graduating with my Associate's Degree in Education and I am already looking at attending Georgia Southwestern University.

This program has changed my life forever. In 2005, I was a high school dropout. In 2020, I became a high school graduate and a college student. In 2022, I will be a college graduate and enrolling into my Bachelor's program at the university. My life will never be the same because of one social media post and one program that gives people who don't have a high school diploma a second chance.

2020 Brittney Marjorie Powell

Good afternoon. My name is Brittney Powell. I have no real direction on writing the perfect speech or saying the right things for it so I'll just start with this. I was that girl who felt regular school wasn't for me. My mom pulled me out in eighth grade to homeschool me but I was sadly defiant in my younger years and really did not take it seriously. I married by seventeen and from there tried a few different approaches to further my education and achieve a high school diploma. I enrolled into GED school but found there again I couldn't grasp the way they rushed through each class and again I gave up and shut the door on it. I wanted an education and the right to say yes I too have a diploma but I couldn't seem to find anything that worked. I couldn't find the help I needed. I was just stuck and accepted I wasn't going to ever really finish school or wear a cap and gown.

Then one day a door was opened to me by a friend and from there she introduced me to Dr. Mabry. My life right then took a beautiful spiral and bam I was doing high school again. Dr. Mabry treated me like I matter but honestly, she treats everyone that way. Even when life became hard and I hit a rough personal patch, this lady and my mother would not let me give up. She stayed on me to not give up. She held me accountable. She and my mother in the background were cheering me on. Part of doing schooling and succeeding is having teachers that care for you ... I have certainly had this. Even if you are there alone doing your work, Dr. Mabry and my mom were only a message or phone call away. No matter how busy they were, all I needed to say was help and I had it.

But this isn't just about me, it's about us all. We made it, class of 2020! Even when the world turned upside down we pushed forward. Reached our goals and now here we stand, diploma in hand. We may have to sit six feet apart, cover our faces, and wear gloves, but it is worth it! We have showed everyone that no matter what, we did not give up!

Matthew 7:7-8 says, "Ask, and it will be given to you; seek, and you will find; knock, and it will be opened to you. For everyone who asks receives, and the one who seeks finds, and to the one who knocks it will be opened."

This verse speaks volumes to me and all that I feel we have endured to get right here where we are! I want to say thank you first to the good Lord. Through you only is all this possible. Thanks to my parents—you have been and are my biggest fans. Thank you to my husband. I love you and you have worked and paid bills so I could get right here standing where I am today. And then thank you Dr. Mabry. You took a dream of a small-town girl and made it a reality. You have been the pillar that holds the walls from crumbling for us all. You have given up your life for all of us. Not just me but my fellow classmates and those still waiting to be right here where we are right now. How do you repay someone like you who is priceless? I can't pay you your worth in gold. I can't even have the time to explain what an amazing, selfless woman you truly are. Those who know you like I have learned to know you already know. We should all strive to have the heart you have. Class of 2020, friends, and family, we have done it! Please join me in giving Dr. Mabry and ourselves a round of applause and thank you!

2021 Rachel Wall

Wow. It feels very surreal to be here today. A long time ago I decided this wasn't going to be something I ever experienced. It feels very refreshing to prove myself wrong like this. Thank you Heidi for the connection.

Growing up in my childhood home was very stressful. Going to school was hard because my education came after all of the other needs of our family were met. Which really meant that none of my academic needs got met. So I kept falling behind.

After dropping out, I attempted to find information about getting my GED a few times. I would always end up in a similar mental space of making excuses as to why I couldn't go through with it. I had a hard time finding information about classes and cost. Truthfully, I had the hardest time finding the confidence I needed to move forward on my own. I spent years procrastinating and avoiding furthering my own education.

It wasn't until a wonderful friend of mine named Heidi Cloud began to push me to go back to school that anything changed. Heidi believed in me and saw potential in me a long time before I did. After I started the program, my confidence increased with every class I completed. Her support, taking her time to find the alternative program for me, and setting me up with Dr. Mabry are the reasons I am here today.

The alternative diploma program was such a different experience. I enjoyed being able to pick my classes and my pace. Although the program did have set deadlines, I was able to set personal goals for myself and meet them, which really helped with my confidence and drive. The design of the program worked well for me. The setup of making sure I understood the material instead of just pushing me through was really helpful. If I missed something or didn't understand a concept right away, I really appreciated how the program reviewed material and quizzes, making sure I was on-pace and confident going into my test. My belief in myself and my ability to learn and what I could do began to skyrocket from there.

Since finding the alternative diploma program, my life changed.

Everyone has shown me so much kindness and support.

I'm still in shock when I think about the moment when I found out that I received a scholarship from the Georgia Independent Auto Dealers Women's Auxiliary Fund. I was over the moon. The idea that people I didn't even know wanted to help me complete the program was life changing and further showed me there is no limit to what I can do. Taking that financial stress off my back was a tremendous help to me and my family.

During the program I took many science classes, such as environmental science and biology, and I fell in love. The first science class I took was physical science and I talked about the class to anyone who would listen for weeks. I'd never been so excited to learn in my life. I knew early on that these classes really held my interest and would be something I would want to pursue in the future.

This program didn't just give me a high school diploma—it gave me an opportunity to transform my entire future.

This program also rewrote the academic history of my family. I am the first sibling to graduate with a high school diploma. I am very excited to announce I have been accepted to Central Georgia Technical College. I will begin to pursue an Associate in science this summer. I am so grateful for all the kindness and support I have received over the past few years.

---------- Forwarded message --------- From: Rachel Wall

Date: Mon, May 1, 2023 at 10:52 AM Subject: Update

To: Annise Mabry <DrMabry@tiersfreeacademy.org>

Good morning Dr. Mabry, I'm not sure if you remember me. I graduated from your program a few years ago. I wanted to let you know I am graduating from Gwinnett Technical College with my Associate in Applied Science this month. Thank you so much for helping me achieve this. Your program had such a positive influence on life and I just wanted to share my gratitude.

With love, Rachel Casey

2021 Stephanie Johnson

Growing up, elementary school was very challenging in the first few years because I was dealing with bullying from my peers. I was bullied for my moles which resulted in me not feeling confident. I also experienced some trauma from a family member. My grandfather sexually assaulted me, which resulted in me—an all A and B honor roll student—getting Fs. But I moved past that era by taking therapy and confiding in my mom and sister. I also made friends who went through similar experiences so we healed together by talking through our feelings. As my childhood school years are coming to an end, I can say that school was very fun and an experience to say the least.

When we first started homeschooling, my mom used Connections Academy. Even though this school was online, it wasn't a good fit for me. That's when my mom found out about the Tiers Free Academy homeschool program.

This program differs from any school that I've entered and I was impressed by the structure of the program. For example, I love the fact that students have a whole month to finish one class and on their own time. I also think the program is very well thought out. Let's say a student is having a bad mental health day. They won't be penalized for it as long as they communicate with their course instructors. This allows students to be successful despite setbacks.

The hardest thing about the diploma program in my opinion, is staying on top of your work because it is very easy to fall off track with the amount of freedom that is provided to us. But being able to work four hours a day is your true pathway to success. My advice to other students would be to buy some nice notebooks because writing things down is a better way to help you learn rather than typing up everything. I'd also tell other students to NOT procrastinate. Lastly, do not be afraid to reach out for help. Your instructors are there to answer all questions. I understand being shy but you'd better be safe than sorry. Sometimes it's hard to believe that I am graduating on May 15, 2021. I am thinking about applying to Atlanta Institute of Music and Media. I would attend for a year and get a feel for the undergraduate school atmosphere and get my Associate's degree. I would then apply to a four-year university or go discover life. I am very interested in UCLA and Emory (SOM). UCLA has the best gymnastics team and I want to put my flexibility and talents to good use. Emory School of Medicine on the other hand has perfect opportunities for me to work in the medical field. I am a caring person and very nurturing so I'd like to put that to use for others.

Update: Stephanie was accepted to both Payne University and Georgia State University in 2024. She is currently attending Georgia State University.

2022 Jessica Stewart
Rockdale County Graduation

Good morning family, friends, community leaders, and fellow graduates, the first thing I want to say is WE MADE IT! There are so many moments that happened today that I honestly didn't think I would ever get to experience—like zipping up my graduation gown, decorating my cap, and most importantly, standing here in front of you delivering a graduate reflection speech.

Growing up, school was really a challenge for me. I found it difficult to focus on learning and to do my work independently with so many other students in the class. I found myself getting lost in my own head a lot, and it felt like I was never on task and constantly trying to catch up.

Honestly, what I truly needed was more individual support, more one-on-one help. That's what made it easier for me to learn. However, the reality is that it's not always possible for teachers to be able to give that one-on-one help with large class sizes (and yes, I know some people say that twenty-five to twenty-eight students in a single class isn't that large).

Maybe for students who don't struggle, it's not an issue. But to be one student in a sea of twenty-eight with a teacher who is spread thin and five students with a hand in the air asking for help—it's just so hard. English was that class for me. Year after year, I struggled. Every year it happened to be the class with the most students, the class where I'd have the least amount of support when I needed it. Every year, I struggled my way through English, feeling lost. My parents did everything in their power to help me to be successful. They even tried putting me in private school, but I still dropped out.

That's what most people don't understand about students who drop out of school. We don't drop out because we aren't trying our best. We drop out because we are trying our best and still not succeeding. We are giving it everything that we have and we are still not making any progress.

When my parents first found Tiers Free Academy, I thought it was going to be another failure of a school experience for me. But after speaking with Dr. Mabry, I knew this was going to be different, because right off the bat I felt more comfortable. Before this moment, "comfortable" was never a word that I would use to describe how I felt going to school. I felt confident and positive about going because I was going to be able to work at my own pace. I felt confident knowing that there were videos I could access if I didn't understand something from the lecture or wanted to review. I even had access to extra lessons with new examples if I needed more support. Yet the best part was that I could do all my classes on my phone—I wasn't stuck in front of a computer or forced to sit in a classroom.

For the first time, I felt like it was almost a guarantee that I would be successful. For the first time, it didn't seem like going to school would place this massive mental strain on me. My happiest moment was when we got the call that I was being accepted into the program. It was like a breath of fresh air.

Now, just because the program felt like a breath of fresh air didn't mean that it was going to be easy. In fact, the hardest part of the program for me was my English 4 class. I had only needed three classes to graduate. I finished the other two quickly, but once again, I found myself stuck in English.

But this time was different. In my previous schools and classes, when I would get stuck in Language Arts or English, I would end up so frustrated with trying to figure it out. But not this time. This time I had someone who saw me. Dr. Mabry saw me, even when she wasn't in the same room as me.

I'm standing here today because my parents never gave up on me, and because I finally had a teacher who not only saw me but who also believed in me. Now that I am a high school graduate, I'm proud and excited to say that I'm going to do something that I never dreamed possible—I'm going to college. I plan on studying Criminal Justice at a technical college then transferring to a four year university to complete my degree. My dream job is to become a hostage negotiator.

As I look to my future and being one step closer to my dream job, I know it's becoming a reality because I've earned my high school diploma. I don't know where I would be without the Tiers Free Academy program, and I'm grateful for all the opportunities it has opened for me.

2022 Deneen Evette Porter

In 1981, I was a student at D.F. Douglass Elementary. I remember feeling scared my first day there. I was walking to my kindergarten class with my niece when we parted ways and she left for her own class. I realized I didn't know anyone. That was when I first met my teacher, Mrs. Patricia Green. I remember crying while she held me close to her all day, and eventually, as the days passed, things got better for me. I made friends along the way.

Years later, when I entered high school, the work became more serious but it was still fun. I loved learning and being engaged. I joined the Marching Band and Chorus because I knew that these two classes would give me the chance to travel and go places. It was entertaining and fun to hang out with classmates and friends. I had days where I struggled with work and days where I had to ask for help, but I always put forth my best effort.

Everything changed for me when I entered the eleventh grade. That year, my mom was diagnosed with ovarian cancer and I later ended up pregnant. It felt as though the world had turned against me. I remember feeling ashamed. Among my siblings, I was the youngest and still living at home, so I did what I had to do. I made sure my mom made it to all of her doctors' appointments and chemotherapy treatments. On top of that I was struggling with morning sickness, from what felt like morning to noon to night. I felt I had given up after the birth of my first daughter, and just ten months later, my mom passed away. As the years passed, I was often ashamed of what others thought of me. There were also days when I just didn't care what anyone thought of me. So I stayed away. I avoided people, school functions, reunions, and graduations.

As the years passed, I decided to get my GED, so I enrolled in GED classes. I realized as I was getting older that it was becoming more difficult for me to find employment without a diploma. I took a couple parts of the GED testing and passed. Then I got pregnant again with my second daughter, and again I stopped going to the classes. By the time I was ready to return after having her, things had changed. I was told I had to start over. I tried to take the new GED a few times but I struggled to pass the tests.

In 2019, I heard about the Macon County Chiefs' Diploma program through a friend. I had to fight just to get my transcript, because my old high school had closed and they hadn't done a good job of transferring the old records. I ended up having to use my old report cards as record for the classes I had taken and still needed since there was nothing on file with the county from my high school. When I learned I only needed two classes to graduate, I honestly didn't think it would work out for me, since everything had advanced and technology had changed tremendously since I was younger. But after witnessing my sister and others achieve their goals, I realized I had to reevaluate myself and what I wanted.

I decided to go for it. I enrolled in the two classes, but it was my first time taking an online course, so I was scared. Fortunately, with the help of my family and friends, as well as the encouragement from Chief Patricia Barber and Dr. Annise Mabry, I finished! To everyone who encouraged me to stay the course, I'm standing here today to say thank you all!

This program was nothing like GED classes. As I worked from the privacy of my own home, I realized how perfect this was for me. I was in my comfort zone and never felt ashamed to ask questions or seek help. It wasn't judgmental.

The hardest thing for me when it came to the diploma program was making sure I stayed on task to finish in time to graduate with the class of 2022. I am a full-time employee at Company Keepers LLC out of Kathleen, Georgia, where I work as a Certified Nurse's Assistant. It was difficult to juggle work, my household, and school. This time was different though because I was determined not to give up.

Now that I've reached this milestone, it doesn't stop here. I will be enrolling in the fall at South Georgia Technical College in Americus, Georgia to study nursing. It's the beginning of a new journey for me. It is as God said: "The race is not given to the swift but to those who endure to the END."

2022 John Andrades Baisden

Well, growing up I wasn't a part of the public school system like most people understand or can relate to. I was homeschooled. Educationally speaking, the curriculum was not unlike the public system, but it did allow me to learn and grow at my own pace. We still were able to participate in afterschool activities and social programs, which helped with social relationships. Overall, I value my experience as a homeschooler. But as I got older, I just didn't see the value of being a homeschool graduate because it didn't have all of the public graduation fanfare of a traditional high school graduation, so I lost my focus. I did try to obtain my GED in the past. However, sometimes in life we end up with a lot on our proverbial plate which was where I found myself.

Working a job, managing relationships, and doing what I could to maintain myself made further educational efforts difficult.

I was referred to the Macon County Chiefs' Diploma Program by a friend. I was a bit skeptical at first because I had previously tried but it didn't work out. This friend was able to explain the vast difference that this program had as opposed to others. I stepped out on a wild leap and made the decision to try again. It worked! Thankfully, this program has influenced not only people I know but now, I can include myself as well.

This program was different because unlike most GED programs, it did not require students to attend regular classes at some point. If you have any conception of what it's like to work and manage a home life you would know that it's nearly impossible. This program allowed me to work and study at the available times that I had. Much like homeschooling, this program also allowed me to learn at my own pace, so I wasn't ever worried about falling behind. It's been great to fulfill my aspirations to achieve my diploma.

The flexibility of this program was the greatest impact for me.

Being able to work my way to a diploma while not failing as a parent or employee was an all-around benefit. The style in which this program was created was thoughtful in the way that it was created for real people with lives to live. That alone has been very impactful on my education. The results are real and evident to my family and friends. I know that sometimes life doesn't happen the way we want it to happen. I know how hard it is to say those four words—I need my diploma. I know that fear and hesitation can be demotivating but I want to say to you today: don't hesitate any longer. There is a way for you to obtain your diploma without making harsh or life-altering decisions. This is a program for you that can fit any life situation—now I didn't say this program was easy because it's not an easy program, but it is an achievable program if you focus on the class in front of you. Stop putting off what you really want because of those "what ifs" in your life. Stop living your life through your rearview mirror and live your life looking through your windshield. Rearview mirrors are smaller for a reason. What is behind you is small when you look at what's in front of you.

What is in front of me as a high school graduate is more than I can explain in words. First, this will allow me to take the next step in life and go for my B.A. in fire science. I'm a firefighter by trade and a major factor in my occupation is always to further my education. This will not only benefit the community I serve but my family as well. Pay increases and promotions are all based on educational standings. So, the rest of my life and career are being built upon by my high school diploma.

Update: In December 2023, John Baisden graduated with his Associate's Degree from Albany Technical College. In 2024, John obtained his Emergency Medical Technician (EMT) Certification and is in the process of completing his Georgia Registry exams to obtain his license.

2022 Shentoria Baisden

Growing up, school was always fun for me. It was where I could talk with my friends, learn different things and attend field trips. My teacher was also a parent to me, as I was homeschooled, which has had a way of bringing out more artistic creativity in my abilities to learn and grow. It worked because I was someone who learned in a different way than public systems teach. There are life lessons to be learned everywhere, I suppose, but I learned so much from being homeschooled, including some things that weren't taught in traditional classrooms. Overall, it was a great educational journey for me.

I had been searching for a program for a while and had researched a number of programs when I found the Macon County Chiefs' Diploma Program. I had first heard about the diploma program through a mutual friend, but when it came to reaching out, I kept putting it off. I didn't think any more about it for a while.

This was because I had attempted to earn my diploma in the past and struggled to be successful. It's not that I wasn't ready for it, but rather, that the circumstances surrounding my life made it impossible for me to get there at the time. I had a hard time finding a program with specific classes that would align with my situation in life. When I finally did, it was with this program, and I am so grateful for how this program is designed.

It worked for me. I found it to be more centered on helping me obtain my diploma while still being able to function as a parent and a full-time employee. I found other programs too rigorous and structured, to the point where it was impossible to maintain my life schedule while furthering my education at the same time. This program has been a blessing in a way that will benefit everyone in my life, not just me.

The level of support that I received in this program was also different from anything else I had found. Chief Barber was always friendly, helpful, and had so many encouraging words to share. Whenever I spoke with Chief, I always felt I had the support that kept me driven and motivated, believing I could accomplish my dreams. This support, along with the attention to detail and flexibility of the program, truly impacted me on an interpersonal level. Watching my family express their happiness with my academic growth has changed my outlook on everything in my life. It is something I will never forget.

To anyone thinking about getting their diploma or struggling with it, I encourage you to not hesitate any longer. Whatever your excuse or situation, take the leap of faith. Put yourself through this program. Earning your diploma is not as far away as you may think, and this program will help you change the outcome for the rest of your life. It was a step out of my complacent comfort zone, but it was worth it! I think about the fact that I am going to be a high school graduate, and it means everything to me. Life dreams that I've always wanted to see fulfilled are now within my reach. They're coming true! I was always hard on myself for never completing high school, but now I can say that I've finished a long-awaited obstacle. I stand here knowing that my kids can see that Mommy is so happy, and they see what I've accomplished now. I've shown them that nothing can slow you down if you refuse to let it.

I know this program is operated by grant funds, and I also want to express my gratitude to the grant funders for having invested in me. The funding you've provided to this program I will utilize for the rest of my life. You didn't just change my life; your support of this program changed the life of my entire family.

Now that I am a high school graduate, I plan to attend college to work on my Associate's Degree. I plan to work in the public service field, with my ultimate goal to become a probation officer, where I can help others get their life back on track. I've thought about this goal for years now, and I'm finally moving towards it.

Earning my high school diploma has been one of the most significant milestones in my life. I've made it, and everything from here on out is pushing me upward!

Update: In December 2023, Shentoria Baisden obtained her Associate's Degree from Albany Technical College in Early Childhood Education and is currently pursuing her Bachelor's Degree in Early Childhood Education.

2022 Rashad Jones "My Journey to a High School Diploma"

Growing up, school was feasible yet challenging for me. It was a bit difficult for me to juggle life and schoolwork all at once and having multiple distractions did not help either. Although it was hard, it made me very aware of my strengths and weaknesses. I used that to improve myself as a student and all-around person. It was a process, but I gave myself a lot of grace and patience in the face of adversity. I stopped attending school due to responsibilities. I worked two jobs to help my mom around the house financially. Although I was lightening the load around the house, I felt as if I had let everyone down including myself. Everyone looked up to me in our household and I felt as if I was not leading by example. My mom tried to use homeschool programs to help me but I just wasn't focused enough at the time to put in the effort to finish the work. It made me feel disappointed in myself.

I learned about the alternative diploma program through a family member. After talking with my aunt about how I felt after stopping school, she encouraged me to re-enroll. It was a team effort. My family and I did some research, made some phone calls, and used our best judgment to decide what was best for me.

See, I had been fighting to become a high school graduate for a long time. I attempted to get my GED twice and it was extremely draining for me. Getting up for class after a long night of work was difficult. I felt like I was not giving it my all due to being so tired. While attending class, I was mentally and physically unavailable. I knew I was capable of so much more, but life just kept getting in the way.

The GED program that I was enrolled in was very structured and inflexible. In my experience, it really wasn't designed for working adults, but the alternative diploma program was different. The diploma program gave me a chance to move at my own pace. It provided me with my own personal learning environment. I completed my assignments with ease when working, and it gave me a chance to relax while learning. Because of this, it was a lot less challenging for me to retain information and focus. It was also very convenient for me, making it easier to juggle school and work at the same time. I have not regretted my decision at all.

Being my own teacher was the most challenging thing for me. Completing the assignments was the easy part but teaching myself with deadlines included made me a bit anxious. Self-taught courses were out of my comfort zone, but this showed me a new strength I possessed. It made me proud of myself and showed me I can do anything that I put my mind to. This program helped to build my character in a sense of never doubting myself.

Being a high school graduate will grant me the level of comfort that I have always wanted. I plan to join the military, Army to be exact. This will aid me tremendously in providing for my two boys and myself. Not only will there be financial gains, but there will also be emotional gains as well. This is a long overdue legacy that will be fulfilled. My mom graduated at the top of her class. Now, her son will be graduating with two double honor cords.

2022 Michael Lynn McGhee Jr.

Growing up, school life was characterized by a mix of challenges and good times. Despite the challenges, I was an active student in class and school activities. Most of the teachers had a soft spot for me. In academics, I fared well with average performances. The subject that gave me a difficult time was mathematics, but I overcame it with time. In co-curriculum activities, I was an active member of the marching band in middle and high school. I can use many words to describe school life, but the most specific words are endurable and wonderful. I can describe myself as a sociable person while growing up and in school. I made many friends who had a minimum knowledge of who I was. We had a lot of fun and engaged in many activities that gave us good memories from school.

From a social point of view, I lost myself in the conundrum of having too many social relations that fueled my distancing from focusing on school. My attention was divided between social life and school life. Eventually, my social life won the race. Many friends did not even know simple facts about me, like my favorite color, meal, or even my worst feeling. The truth is that I liked it that way. I did not like people knowing too much about me, as I could easily detach from the relationship whenever I wanted. These became the sources of my downfall; I lost my focus in school. My performance started to decline at an intolerable rate. I could not even explain to my parents what was going wrong. I got discouraged due to low self-esteem as I would not say I liked the pressure of seeing poor performance and enjoyed the company of too many friends who performed better than me.

I had tried getting my GED in the past. However, I faced some serious setbacks along the way. Due to distance, I did not have proper time management to attend the program effectively. This deprived me of my motivation and morale for the program. Money was another problem. There were times when I did not have the money to commute to the program or the financial support to maintain other areas of my life so that I could focus on getting my GED. Even if the program was offered in an area with public transportation, I did not have bus fare to get there.

Consequently, even if I could walk to the institution, I could not make it on time due to the distance. Therefore, I lacked the self-drive I have today, which led me to be reluctant and conservative about pushing forward with the program. Hence, I was not able to obtain my GED.

I know someone would tell me that I should have sought assistance. Nevertheless, I was too discouraged and soaked in low self-esteem to approach anyone for help. The journey seemed more complicated and more challenging to continue than to stop. Quitting won the race.

I would describe my ability to obtain employment without a high school diploma as a challenging adventure. It is straightforward to locate vacancies, but a high school diploma requirement limits the chances of securing employment to a bare minimum or none. The jobs are generally available, but the filtering requirement is when a high school diploma transcript or proof of a high school diploma is required. I have made numerous applications only to be told that having a high school diploma is the minimum requirement. Further- more, the massive discouragement comes from the fact that it is not the main requirement but the minimum requirement, among others. I have always ended up pulling out of the race due to that. It is an essential document in searching for employment, particularly when employers require it. Hence, my ability is reduced to almost none to secure any job without a diploma as proof of qualification. It is challenging to secure a spot when one lacks the document. It was also equally frustrating to hear people say that jobs were readily available if people wanted to work but what many people do not understand is that there are a lot of adults without a high school diploma who want to work, but companies cannot hire them because they do not have the minimum entry requirement of a high school diploma.

I learned about the Rural Communities Diploma Program from a colleague at work. As we were conversing with him and his wife, they mentioned an option to get a high school diploma, and it wasn't a GED. They felt that this program could benefit me immensely. They told me they knew of several people who took the program successfully and secured jobs after completing it. Their words captured my attention and triggered my curiosity. I eventually researched it online and got to know more about the program.

That is how I managed to learn about the alternative diploma program. The two sources provided all the necessary information and all I needed to know about the program. I even asked friends about the program because it did not seem real, and the feedback was positive. They motivated me to take it and ensured that I took it seriously. All these gave me many reasons to enroll in the program and ensure that I did my best to complete the course and earn my diploma. The program has some unique aspects that make it so different. One of the significant aspects is the opportunity it gives the participants to attend and finish their high school diploma program without spending much time in the institution. The program is flexible in scheduling and everything is online. The lessons are well-timed and brief. Having a quiz at the end of the lesson helps because you don't have to go all the way through the course only to have your entire grade determined by two or three exams. Because it's online, there is less pressure to not miss classes due to daily class attendance. The program also has minimal pressure on students on assignment completion and submission. It is, therefore, a different program that suits my needs and preferences. I can do my work under no pressure and handle other tasks along with the program. I cannot emphasize more how the program is suitable for anyone who wishes to take it. From an honest point of view, I have not found anything difficult about the program. It suits anyone who has a positive attitude and is consistent in the classwork. After some time, I realized that my procrastination trait was the barrier keeping me from signing up. I had to stop procrastinating to sign up and make the move to approach the institution to get started. The process is straightforward, and all that one needs is the self-drive to decide when to get started. The decision to sign up and get started is all that one needs to make to hit the ground running.

There are no demands or restrictions that make the program difficult. However, that does not mean that there are no rules. The program has simple rules and policies that are easy to follow and adhere to. It was not an easy journey during the first trial, but after I took my chances, I completed the program and earned my diploma. For sure, challenges are inevitable, and for the program, the challenges one experiences are not considerable or significant enough to make the program challenging.

To anyone afraid to take the first step in acquiring a high school diploma, there are a few things I would advise you. First, choose to take the program and do not look back. Do not look around or procrastinate; decide to take the program. Secondly, challenges are inevitable and come unexpectedly anywhere at any time. Therefore, do not give up. Just keep on pushing and pushing beyond those limits, and you will make it to the end. Thirdly, embrace focus and consistency. Do not let bad social settings or friends encourage poor habits that do not positively influence your future academically. I made a mistake, and I would not advise anyone to make the same mistake. I do not advise you not to have friends, but to have friends who support your dreams. The good thing about having a small circle of friends is that there is minimal peer pressure and social expectations to push you to the wrong side. Embrace that perspective and ensure that you do not look back or around, as it might be a source of discouragement.

Update: Michael Lynn McGhee Jr. is working as a law enforcement officer in Georgia.

2023 Guadalupe Benitez Paredes

Good morning fellow classmates, elected officials, family and friends, it feels great to be standing here today. I never imagined that my essay would be selected as a graduation reflection essay. My journey from where I started to this very moment (standing here in front of you) has been a long and arduous one.

What do they say about not valuing what you have until you lose it? I stopped attending school in the eighth grade and as I got older, my focus shifted from school to social life. I made the terrible decision to stop attending school to hang around friends. Gradually, I started missing school a lot. And time runs when you are out of school wasting away as I soon realized that I had made the worst decision possible.

I would see students getting off to school after I stopped attending and I'd miss school so much. I missed learning and the interaction. All this academic nostalgia encumbered my mind with regrets and great sadness. I missed about a year or two and thought it was too late to return to school. I thought I would be much older than the students in the grades I left off. But again, I was wrong, I should have researched different school options. I never returned to school.

I later enrolled in GED classes for a few months. To be honest, I really loved the feeling of learning again during my time attending classes. It felt good to be in school again. Unfortunately, work became a hindrance and I began to miss classes due to my work schedule.

Eventually, I gave up. My greatest barrier to learning in my GED classes was fear and a not so positive view of adult education.

I became very skeptical about returning to finish my high school diploma because of my fear of failing and completing the course. My experience with the GED program further reinforced this fear and solidified my belief that all adult education programs were the same. I believed that I was too old to learn and succeed and I felt I'd be a disengaged learner from the start. I remember when I first started at Tiers Free Academy. I was so scared that I was going to fail again. But Tiers Free offered the right resources and support to help me overcome this fear. So, I developed a purpose for engaging in the learning experience and succeeding, and part of this purpose was my daughter—Gloria.

With a defined purpose, I was no longer afraid of failing because I made the necessary changes in my life. This allowed me to focus on my goals. I'd also become more disciplined and patient. These were particularly helpful traits in my journey to achieving a high school diploma. Failure ceased to be an option because aside from my motivation to succeed, the program was also different.

My biggest motivation and supporter for enrolling in the diploma program is my daughter Gloria. She is nine years old and in the fourth grade. I mentioned to her the opportunity I was exposed to through this program and she was excited. She asked if I would be attending the local high school. I explained to her that although I may look sixteen, my age will not allow me to enroll. After the completion of each course, we'd sit down and log each course.

This was a special moment we shared together and it reminds me to keep going and not give up. I constantly remind my daughter the importance of completing school. I want my daughter to have the skills to choose any career she is interested in. I want to be an example for her. I want to show my daughter it is never too late to work towards your goals.

Now, even though my goal is greater and a lot scarier, I refuse to fail because failure is no longer an option for me. I'm confident and committed to do whatever it takes to achieve my goal of completing college. I want to continue to learn and find a field where I'm able to feel fulfilled after a long day. To my fellow classmates, I want y'all to know that our education doesn't stop here. I want us to continue our education after this program. Some of us are parents and we need to be a leading light and example for our kids, a reminder (via our actions) that education unlocks doors of opportunities.

Some of us have been looking at closed doors of opportunities for a long time. I know this because I personally looked at closed doors for half of my adult life but not anymore. Today, I am a high school graduate and I finally have the key to unlocking my future. It is often said that education is power and true leaders lead by doing and not dictating. I've always wanted to be a shining example for my kids and I'm positive that my pursuit of further education will enable me to become this great example.

On a final note, I want to use this opportunity to thank the Atlanta Redemption Ink for opening the door to give me access to enroll at the Tiers Free Academy. I want to specially appreciate Dr. Mabry for the insight to create this noble program. To my family, I say thank you for the overwhelming support. I'm pleased to announce that I want to further my knowledge in the field of information technology so I can advance my current career. I am currently a system support specialist.

In the words of Anthony J. D'Angelo, "Develop a passion for learning. If you do, you will never cease to grow."

2023 Tiara Holmes "Foster Care Is Failing but I'm Graduating"

Good morning staff, elected officials, friends, families, and my fellow classmates. My name is Tiara Holmes and I am currently in foster care. My placement in foster care didn't dictate my pathway in life. Now, the statistics say that I shouldn't be standing here in front of you today because only 4 percent of children in foster care in Georgia graduate from high school.

But here I am. Not only as a high school graduate but also as a student graduation reflection speaker. This is both an honor and an opportunity. Thank you to the 2023 Graduation Speaker Committee for selecting me.

I'm not going to give you lots of well-researched information. Research is good but today, I want to talk to you about my reality. My reality is I have been navigating through the foster care system all my life. No system is perfect but the foster care system in Georgia is broken. It is broken when it comes to making sure that we have basic life skills such as opening a bank account to receive a paycheck or building our credit as teenagers so that we can get an apartment. It is broken in how we are treated by the caseworkers, the courts, and the foster families. Our voices are always silenced and we are seen as the problem and not as children caught in a broken, problematic system.

The Georgia foster care system is broken but it didn't break me. My reality is I am getting a chance to graduate from high school because I had access to a program that most other foster care kids don't have. The truth is I wouldn't be standing here in front of you as a high school graduate if not for a chance to participate in this homeschool program.

Growing up, I loved learning but getting to school was hard and staying focused when I was at school was even harder. My reality is I never really had a support system or anybody that believed in me. So I learned quickly to only depend on myself.

As I bounced from foster homes to group homes, it was hard to keep myself motivated to do my school work. I was given the label of a problematic orphan but honestly I was just a child who needed someone to listen. I never had a stable learning environment when it came to attending school. So school was always an interruption in my life that was already chaotic.

One of the biggest problems that I experienced as a foster child was the amount of time that it would take for me to get enrolled in school once I arrived at a new home. It would sometimes take weeks for my records to arrive at the school. I lost a lot of time taking classes I already finished and this caused me to miss the classes that I needed. When I stopped attending school, I thought about a GED but I didn't want that. My twin sister graduated from high school and my parents always told me a GED was not as good as a high school diploma. I honestly felt that way too. My goal was always to get a high school diploma, no matter how I got it. All I wanted was for my twin sister to see me walk across the stage as a high school graduate just like she did.

Nothing about my life has been easy. But life without a high school diploma, it was almost impossible. I found it very hard to apply for jobs. I doubted myself after not being able to finish high school. I just experienced so many major setbacks.

I learned about the Tiers Free Homeschool Diploma program through another program I was attending. I've never been excited about anything when it came to school but for the first time, I was actually quite excited to join this homeschool program.

I remember the first time I talked to Dr. Mabry on the phone about the program. She told me that she had a tribe of people who supported her and her graduates. When I hung up the phone, I thought, "This lady isn't real. There is no way that a tribe of people is going to support students like me." So even though I was hopeful, I didn't want to get my hopes up. I had to remain skeptical to keep from getting hurt.

When she told me I only needed one English class to graduate, I was so excited! For the first time I had the real possibility of being a high school graduate. If I am being honest, homeschool always scared me. I questioned how students would get a proper education attending a homeschool program. How would they genuinely learn from their classes when everything is online and it's so easy to cheat and get by easily? I thought that homeschool meant that you don't really have a social life or get the opportunities to meet new people like the kids who attend public school. I also believed that most homeschool kids lacked communication skills.

I quickly learned that none of this was true. It's not easy to cheat in Dr. Mabry's classes. When Dr. Mabry says, "The only thing I'm giving you is thirty days to complete your class. You earn every single letter on that paper that says High School Diploma," she means it. And if you don't finish that class in thirty days, she will lock you out of the class. The first time it happened to me, I thought she had given up on me just like everyone else always did. The second and third time it happened to me, I started giving up on myself.

It took me five months to complete that one class, but Dr. Mabry did something that no one in my life had ever done for me—she never gave up. No matter how difficult I was. No matter how I talked to her when she tried to encourage me, she never gave up on me. She also didn't hold my hand. She didn't accept my excuses. She expected me to do better but the problem was I didn't expect me to do better. She always told me, "You missed my deadline. Now you tell me how you are going to fix this." She told me that she knew that I was more than capable of doing the work but she didn't have the time or patience to try to feed a student who wasn't hungry to become a high school graduate. I got hungry.

My reality today is I wouldn't be standing here in front of you as a high school graduate if not for this program. I wish this program was available to all of the foster children. As a foster kid, I would've loved to attend this program. I feel like I would've graduated on time. Even though this program had to evaluate my transcript, it didn't take them long to get me enrolled, which was another issue I was dealing with DFCS and the school system. It always took them at least a month to get me in school. A lot of foster kids prefer homeschool because when you think about it, we are already in a pretty bad situation and school just adds more stress on our lives, making us less likely to attend.

I'm finally a high school graduate. My dream is to attend a Historically Black College or University (HBCU) and to major in nursing. I would love to be either an RN or an ER nurse. After I become a nurse, I don't know what I want to do from there but I know for the first time in my life I actually have the tools that I need to determine my future. I now have the ability to create the best life for myself and my child.

2023 Travis Fudge
Rural Communities Diploma Program

Ladies and gentlemen, distinguished guests, and fellow students, I'm Travis Fudge, and I stand before you to share my journey of facing fears and overcoming obstacles in pursuit of becoming a high school graduate.

Growing up, school played a crucial role in shaping my life. It gave me opportunities for education, development, and knowledge acquisition. In 1998, a decision was made to merge the three schools in my county. This decision changed my entire life and eventually caused me to drop out of school.

I didn't want to get a GED because of peer pressure that it was a "Good Enough Diploma." I was not ready to accept it as an alternative to a high school diploma, and societal attitudes at the time reinforced this perspective. But as time went on, I realized I was wrong. I realized how critical it was to question our own assumptions and biases.

Dropping out of high school was a setback, but I refused to let it define the rest of my life. I decided to embrace the idea of homeschooling, but I had to face my biggest fear, the fear of acceptance. Would colleges, universities, and employers recognize the legitimacy of my education? I was consumed by doubt. I knew I needed to find answers, so I began researching. I discovered that homeschooling was not only accepted but also celebrated by educational institutions all over the world.

After this realization, I made a promise to myself to never give up on my education. I vowed to fully commit to finishing my diploma program. I took it as a chance to open doors that were once firmly shut. Before this program, I felt like I was missing out on something big, like a piece of the puzzle that would unlock my true potential. This program feels as if a curtain has been lifted, revealing the world of education that was previously out of my reach.

Growing up, I dreamed of becoming a police officer. I wanted to serve and protect my community. As I got older, so did my ambitions. I looked for different ways to have a bigger impact on society. This inspired me to pursue careers in social justice, community advocacy, or policymaking, where I could address systemic issues while also promoting equity and inclusivity.

This program has breathed new life into me, filling me with hope and endless possibilities. My life has changed in ways I never imagined. The possibilities that now lie before me are vast and inspiring. Higher education, professional advancement, and better job opportunities are all within my reach. More than that, all of my dreams are within reach.

I want to express my gratitude to my wife for her support during this process. She took on many of the household challenges and ensured I would have the necessary resources to succeed. Without her, I would not be standing here today as first a homeschool high school graduate and second as a graduate reflection speaker.

If I could go back in time, I would tell my past self that despite feeling lost and uncertain about the future, you have the strength and resilience to turn things around. I'd tell myself to embrace the journey of self-discovery. Believe in yourself and never underestimate your potential. Take the time to rediscover your passions. You are capable of achieving great things.

To all the adult students out there who are like me, know that you are never alone in your journey. Others have faced challenges and conquered them, and so can you. Shame, fear, and pride are internal prisons that you create for yourself. There is no shame in not having a high school diploma. The shame is not taking advantage of the Macon County Chiefs' Diploma Program to become a high school graduate. Reach out for help and utilize the available resources. Explore alternative learning methods that work for you. It's never too late to pursue your dreams and create the life you envision for yourself. Never forget that greatness awaits those who dare to chase it. Your wildest dreams are within your reach. Trust in your abilities. You are worth the effort.

Thank you and congratulations to all graduates.

2023 Jennika Harris
Rural Communities Diploma Program

I want to start by congratulating all of the graduates. I'm Jennika Harris, and I'm here to tell you that, despite hardship, it's possible to achieve your dreams.

I remember school as more than just a place to learn; it was a place where I could be my true self, meet new friends, and discover the wonders of the world. I enjoyed learning great things about the world and the history of it all. I absolutely loved school, and the experience was amazing!

But my life took an unexpected turn in 2001. I was involved in a terrible car accident that left me shattered physically, mentally, and emotionally for two years. Little did I know that this accident would take away my dream career of becoming a nurse. Not only did the accident rob me of my precious memories, but it also damaged my confidence.

My life is divided into two timelines: my life before the accident and my life after the accident.

Shortly after the accident, I was forced to drop out of school. It pains my heart to not remember anything at all. I often find myself wondering what happened, what went wrong, what I was doing, who did this to me, and why it happened to me.

In 2002, I tried to rebuild my life. I enrolled in GED school but couldn't complete it. Anxiety used to take hold of me in class and this was often triggered by intense stares or questions about the scars on my face or neck. I found myself unprepared to face these challenges, and as a result, my anxiety intensified and hindered my academic progress.

I still get anxious during tests and exams because it's hard to know if I can remember everything. Sometimes I forget small things like my children's birthdays or my own, which is normal for some people. But for me, it causes fear. The fear often makes me question if I should continue my education.

But I'm learning that fear is really False Evidence Appearing Real. I refuse to let it define me. I promised myself that I will face it head-on, not let it overpower me, and that I would not give up. I am grateful for the Macon County Chiefs' Diploma Program because it is giving me my life back. It took a lot of therapy sessions to control my anxiety just so that I'm finally able to go back to school.

I wouldn't be standing here today, delivering this graduation speech, if it weren't for the unwavering support of my father, Willie Harris Sr. He wanted to see me get my high school diploma more than anything. But before I could tell him the good news, we received devastating news that he was dying of pancreatic cancer that had spread to his liver. My world crumbled right in front of my eyes as I stood in his hospital room. But it was then that I made a firm decision to go ahead, work hard, and make him proud.

After finishing high school, I aim to become a medical assistant. I also dream of becoming a cosmetologist. I am committed to making a difference and being a reliable source of support for those who need my services. No matter how difficult the path becomes, I vow to never give up and to continue to be better than yesterday.

If I could go back in time and talk with my past self, I would say, "Don't give up. Keep going and stay focused; you have what it takes, Jennika!" And to all the students who are struggling in school, hear this: You are braver than you believe, stronger than you seem, and smarter than you think. Don't let fear control your life. Stay focused and never lose sight of your dreams.

2023 Keyoshia Sanders

November 9 Graduation Ceremony, Class of 2023

Macon County Rural Communities Diploma Program

Good evening, staff, elected officials, friends, families, and Class of 2023, I want to start by congratulating all of the graduates. I am Keyoshia Sanders, and I want to talk to you about my dreams, my challenges, my reality and how one decision opened up the pathway to an opportunity.

As a kid, I used to dream big about being a police officer. It was all I could think about. But, as I grew up, my dreams went in a different direction, and I ended up wanting to work in early childhood education. I used to be one of those students who genuinely enjoyed school. I had a solid group of friends who shared this journey with me. We motivated each other.

But then came my ninth-grade year, and everything took a sharp turn. My family moved to Warner Robins, and suddenly, I found myself as the new kid in town, with no friends and zero motivation. School went from exciting to boring really quickly, and I felt like an outsider. And you know what made it even worse? I didn't feel like I had the family support I needed to stay on track. I got pregnant but I still kept trying to push myself because in my heart, I knew I needed

a high school diploma.

Fast forward to my senior year, and life took an even tougher turn. I found myself with not one but two kids and I felt the weight of all the responsibility was crushing. So, I made a tough choice that changed the course of my entire life. I made the decision to drop out of school. I had to drop out of school because I felt that I needed to focus on being a mom and working to put food on the table.

I was in survival mode, and what I've learned about living in survival mode is that you don't stop to think about the future. You are simply trying to survive in the moment.

It was a heartbreaking decision, and I couldn't stop feeling regret for not finishing high school. But you know what? I never gave up on my dream of education. I might have dropped out, but I never dropped my determination.

That's when I started looking into alternative paths to finish high school, and I stumbled upon the Penn Foster program. Penn Foster seemed like a great opportunity but the financial aspect got pretty overwhelming quickly. My biggest fear was how I'd juggle the responsibilities of being a young parent while working towards my high school diploma.

My mother kept pushing me to earn the diploma. As I looked at my own children, I was more determined than ever to provide them with a better life. I made a promise to my mom, myself, and my kids that I'd get that high school diploma, no matter the obstacles that lay ahead.

And now, here I am, about to graduate, and let me be honest, it wasn't a piece of cake. Balancing kids, work, and school was far from easy. Thanks to the Rural Communities Diploma Program for providing online classes that fit my hectic work schedule. I understand that this program is possible because of grant funding from the United Way of Greater Atlanta and the International Paper Foundation Flint River Mill. I want these grant funders to know that your grant funding made it possible for me to take the classes without the burden of trying to figure out how I was going to pay for the class. This program turned out to be my game-changer.

People always say, "Pull yourself up by your bootstraps," but these same people don't take the time to realize that some people don't even have boots to grab the bootstraps. Programs like this are the boots AND bootstraps that people like me in rural communities need to become a high school graduate.

If I could go back in time and talk to my younger self four years ago, I'd say, "Don't give up; just finish." If you ever feel like quitting on your dreams, if you're ever thinking about dropping out, don't do it. Hang on a bit longer. Your dreams are just around the corner; wait just enough to see them come true.

Seek help; don't be afraid to ask for support. Talk to your counselor;

reach out to someone who can offer the guidance and encouragement you need. Finish what you started. I promise you, the struggle is worth it, and the sense of accomplishment is like no other.

As I cross this stage and become a high school graduate, I'm not stopping here. I will head back to school and earn a degree in early childhood education. I want to inspire and educate the next generation of little minds.

And who knows—I may even decide to go into the police academy and become a school resource officer with my degree in early child- hood education. For the first time in my life, I've got something that I haven't had for a long time. I have options and opportunities.

The bottom line is to keep chasing your dreams and never, ever give up. It's okay to have setbacks, but it's not okay to quit your dream. The journey may be tough, but the destination is worth every step along the way.

2024 Joy Green "Hidden Homelessness: Rising Above"
Rockdale County Graduation

Congratulations to all the graduates! My name is Joy Green, and I am someone who learned that having a rough start doesn't stop you from having a great finish.

In my early years, I was what you might call a typical nerd—an all-A student, quiet, and admittedly, a little socially awkward. But as the years passed, especially in middle school, something changed. I discovered the joy of cheering, the thrill of friendship, and the comfort of belonging. Life was simple; life was good.

Then came the hardest blow. When I was in twelfth grade, my mom lost her job. In the blink of an eye, our lives changed drastically. We found ourselves without a place to call our own, moving from hotel to hotel and Airbnb to Airbnb until my mother ran out of funds and could no longer figure it out for us.

It was not just me: 2.3 percent of nearly 1.75 million students in our state experienced homelessness last year!

Imagine it—2.3 percent of students wake up every day trying to figure out where they'll sleep while still keeping up with their studies.

2.3 percent of students whose parents are doing everything they can to find some stability in this broken system. Every one of these 2.3 percent has a story, a life, a future that matters.

Suddenly, I was part of that statistic. As I watched my friends thrive in the safety of their homes, my own life felt like a failure. I was sad. I was angry at the unfairness of it all.

How could I sit in class, study, and smile when I didn't even know where I would be sleeping the next night? I could no longer pretend to be happy so my friends wouldn't find out. I walked away from school.

But here's what I held onto—a promise I made to my mother. Despite her own battles with job loss and health issues, she never stopped believing in the power of education, and more importantly, she never stopped believing in me. She always tells me, "One day, you're going to outshine me."

My reality is I never wanted to drop out of school—school was just too much. That's why when my mom and my graduation coach found this program, I seized the opportunity.

This program has lifted me from my lowest points to a place of hope and excitement for a brighter future. On top of that, it allowed me to give my mom the proud moment of seeing me walk across the graduation stage—a moment she's always dreamed of.

Just think about it—if we had more programs like this, imagine how many lives could be turned around! Tiers Free Academy

Homeschool Cooperative has been a lifeline for those of us dealing with homelessness.

As high school ends, I can't wait to start college and pursue my dream of becoming a pediatrician. This path won't be easy, but it's one I'm passionate about and confident in. At the end of the day, that's what truly matters, right?

Today, I'm genuinely proud of how far I've come. There were times when reaching this point seemed utterly impossible. I remember dreaming of walking across the stage with my peers—friends from elementary school—and feeling sad that my path had to be different. But today, I no longer feel that sadness.

In fact, I promise myself that I will never make a permanent decision based on a temporary feeling. I am going to make this a motto I always live by as I navigate through life. There'll be challenges, sure, but also victories, and through it all, I plan to stay true to this promise.

The bottom line is: When resources are limited, let your strength be limitless. Giving up can derail your life in ways you might not expect. Life will challenge you, and throw obstacles in your path that might bring feelings of depression or sadness. Every day, make it a point to rise, show up, and don't give in to them.

2024 Brian Young
Rockdale County Graduation

I want to start by congratulating all of the graduates. My name is Brian Young. From the uncertainties of the first day to the triumphs of this moment, I've travelled the same path as you all.

I hail from the east side of Atlanta, a place where school was more than just academics. It was about surviving the tumultuous environment that surrounded me. Growing up, my siblings and I were no strangers to the spotlight, attracting both positive and negative attention from our peers.

I'll be honest—I didn't always handle the negativity with grace. There were moments when I let it consume me, retaliating in ways that only exacerbated the situation. Besides that, I was always a smart kid. Yet life took an unexpected turn, and circumstances led to a temporary hiatus from public school. It was during this time that my father's dedication kept my education alive at home. When I returned to school two years later, in tenth grade, I had shaky attendance due to a weakened immune system, which caused frequent illness. And if that wasn't enough, I found myself amidst a bad crowd!

Once I started missing school due to these issues, the school threatened to expel me for bad attendance. There were moments when dropping out seemed like the easy way out—a convenient escape from the suffocating pressure. But deep down, I knew I deserved better than that. I knew about the GED, but I wanted to walk across that stage as a high school graduate.

That's when my dad stepped in. He recognized the importance of my education and fought tirelessly for a different pathway to graduation. He kept pushing me, reminding me of all the doors that would open with a diploma in hand. If it were not for him, I would not enroll in this program. So, thank you, Dad, for seeing the potential within me when I had lost faith in myself.

And I would be remiss not to mention the positivity that this program brings to my life. It's transformed my entire outlook on school and reignited my passion for learning. This program has been a game-changer for me.

As I cross this stage and become a high school graduate, I'm not stopping here. After graduation, I plan to attend trade school for my forklift license and barber school after I take a small break from school. During my break, I plan on immersing myself in learning to start a YouTube channel because I've always had big dreams of being famous one day.

I made a promise to myself to bring generational wealth and success to my family, and I'm committed to keeping that promise. Through hard work, positivity, and continuous self-improvement, I'll not only uplift myself but also those around me.

If I could journey back four years, I'd whisper to my past self: "You've got this. Keep your chin up and learn from every stumble." Despite the challenges I faced in school due to external influences, I've learned to let go of those negative memories. Ultimately, I triumphed and graduated. If I hadn't chosen to rise above and distance myself from bad crowds, I wouldn't be where I am today.

To those who may be contemplating dropping out, I urge you to hold on. I know firsthand the attraction of giving up when the going gets tough. But I also know boundless opportunities await on the other side. This program may not be a walk in the park, but it can lead to graduation and beyond.

So, don't listen to whispers of doubt. You are stronger than you realize and more capable than you give yourself credit for. You've got this, and even if it feels like you're alone, know that I'm rooting for you every step of the way! Thank you!

2024 Sir David Elijah Patrick Byron-Dodson

My name is Sir David Elijah Patrick Byron-Dodson and I am someone who dared to reach for a future that once seemed distant.

Growing up, I had a difficult time in school. With a family crisis that forced us to move to a new place, I found myself starting over at a new school. Five such transitions disrupted my academic path. The constant state of being the "new kid" uprooted my ability to form lasting friendships.

Then, the pandemic hit. School became secondary as family crises took center stage. I put my education on hold for two years because I wanted to focus more on my family. When we moved from Boston to Atlanta, it felt like my academic story might just end there—unfinished! But after waiting another year, I started school again. It was a revival of hope, an affirmation that the road could still lead somewhere beautiful. The journey, however, was far from easy.

Being older than most of my classmates, I felt the pressure of time bearing down on me. I had to rush from zero credits to twenty-four to graduate. I had to make up for lost time. I kept thinking I might fail. The burnout was real, and the doubts were constant.

The result? I considered taking the GED exam. But I realized that if I was struggling in school, how could I pass an exam that was meant to test all the knowledge of a high schooler? No, I had to fight through it because I knew that every step was bringing me closer to this moment.

So, I chose a different path. I went to Rockdale Open Campus, where I managed to complete several credits. And what a difference it made! It led me to this very moment of triumph! Now, I'm stepping into a new stage of life with real prospects ahead.

If it weren't for Tiers Free, I might be standing here with an incomplete story. I'd be facing my last semester without the chance to graduate. Thanks to Tiers Free, a huge burden has been lifted—it has opened doors I once thought were permanently closed.

As a homeschool student, my biggest fear was not making something of myself after high school. If high school was this hard, I was concerned about facing bigger challenges ahead. But you know, I decided not to wait for what's next; I chose to actively prepare for it. Once I graduate, my plans are already taking shape. I plan to join the workforce, targeting roles in the automotive industry for experience or in fast food to start saving money. Simultaneously, I'll complete my FAFSA to finance trade school and earn my dream job certifications. I also aim to obtain my CDL and a bachelor's degree in mechanical engineering.

But whatever I end up doing ahead, I promise to give it my all—to honor not only myself but those who have supported me along the way. And I know that to do that, I need to put action behind my words, scale every mountain, and taste success.

If I could speak to my younger self, I'd say: Enjoy the ride, but keep your eyes on the prize. Finish your education decisively, for society has grand plans for you. Tighten up, push forward with no excuses or pleas—just relentless effort and the satisfaction of knowing you've done your utmost to become the best version of yourself.

To those considering dropping out: pause and think—why stop now when you've already come so far? You might doubt the relevance of what you're learning now, but as my credit recovery teacher, Ms. Smith, often says, "Knowledge is like money; it's better to have it and not need it than to need it and not have it."

The real world is tough and doesn't always play fair. With a solid educational foundation, you can not only level the playing field, but you can dominate it as well. Remember, education is a gift that keeps on giving!

2024 Alexa Pulido

Congratulations to all the graduates! My name is Alexa Pulido, and I am someone who dared to grant myself a second chance, a chance that led me to this very moment of triumph.

From a young age, my mother instilled in me the value of education. But as I grew older, I found myself straying from this path. My focus shifted from books to people, from learning to socializing with peers. And as my priorities shifted, so did my academic performance.

Then came the pandemic, and it rocked my academic journey to its core. Imagine being on the brink of ninth grade, buzzing with excitement for the big celebrations and the legendary middle school prom, only to have it all snatched away by COVID. On top of that, I struggled to find motivation to keep going.

The consequences were devastating. I found myself attending ninth grade classes in my tenth grade year. The thought of facing another day in class with people I barely knew was suffocating. I felt isolated, embarrassed, and lost among unfamiliar faces. The once enthusiastic learner in me became disheartened and withdrawn.

And then it happened! I fully stopped attending school in my twelfth grade year. My world was turned upside down when my mother was diagnosed with cancer. I was barely eighteen, faced with the terrifying prospect of losing my mother and navigating life without her guidance. I won't lie—there were times when I thought about giving up, about taking the easy way out.

But I knew that wasn't an option. The thought of dropping out never crossed my mind. While some opted for the GED route, I was resolute in pursuing the traditional path. The open campus seemed like the perfect fit for me, and I thrived within its walls. But my downfall came swiftly, courtesy of my dwindling motivation. I ended up dropping out of high school, isolating myself from my friends, and being forced to homeschool.

It's a weight I've carried for far too long—the regret of not experiencing high school in the way I'd always imagined. I often find myself longing for that picture-perfect school life, filled with cherished memories and milestones. But through it all, I learned valuable lessons. I learned that it's time to release that regret, to let go of the past, and to embrace the present. I accept full responsibility for my decisions. I recognize the repercussions of prioritizing things that ultimately hold little significance. I've come to realize that dwelling on what could have been only holds me back. And most importantly, it's never too late to change your path.

I will never forget the impact this program has had on my life. I never thought I would have the chance for a last opportunity. But beyond all this, it has given me hope that anything is possible if I'm willing to work for it.

Thanks to this program, I rise every morning with an unwavering determination to chase after my lifelong dream of entrepreneurship. After graduation, I'll dive headfirst into cosmetology school. I can't wait to become a skilled, licensed nail technician. I do it not just for myself but for the future I envision—a future where I am empowered, successful, and truly living life on my own terms. With my mom by my side, I know I can accomplish anything.

So, to those of you who are ready to give up, I urge you—don't. The value of a high school diploma is immeasurable. It opens doors to countless opportunities and serves as a stepping stone to a brighter future. Abandoning it now would be selling yourself short. Graduating alongside your peers is something I'd tell you not to compromise on—it's a milestone worth striving for, without regret. If you're struggling, don't hesitate to seek help. Your future self will thank you for it.

The world awaits, and I have no doubt that each and every one of you will go on to achieve greatness.

2024 Elijah Weston-Vaughn
Rockdale County Graduation

My name is Elijah Weston-Vaughn. My life's journey has been a testament to resilience, a relentless battle against the odds imposed by the foster care system.

Born into a world that seemed to bet against me, I navigated a labyrinth of foster homes, each move eroding my connection to stability and education. The system, designed for protection, became my adversary, and I found myself lost in its shadows.

Misunderstood, I was branded and dismissed by those who failed to look beyond my struggles. The culmination of seven years of fighting against a relentless current led me to question the very purpose of my education.

At sixteen, I faced a crossroads and chose to step away from traditional schooling. Who wouldn't seek an escape from such unyielding hardship?

My experiences have unveiled harsh truths about foster care: the direct path it paves to incarceration, the dismal graduation rates, and the educational setbacks with each transition. These aren't mere statistics; they represent stifled dreams and uncertain futures.

Today, I stand before you, not as a product of the system, but as a disruptor of the foster care to prison pipeline.

In the chaos, my father, C'dric Vaughn, was my beacon of hope. His unwavering belief in me fueled my potential. His passing left an irreplaceable void, yet his legacy propels me forward. My stepmother, Tania, with her mantra of taking life "one step, one day at a time," introduced me to a diploma program that promised more than accreditation—it promised hope.

Here I am, a living tribute to my father's memory, embodying the very essence of his belief in progress, one step at a time. Despite the fear of failure and the daunting prospect of missed opportunities, I refused to succumb to the fate of a statistic. Supported by a family that saw my worth, and grandparents who championed my every move, I chose to rise.

My narrative isn't meant for comfort; it's a call to action. It's a plea for acknowledgement that existing programs are failing students like me. It's a plea for elected officials and community leaders to not only acknowledge the life altering impact that Tiers Free Academy Homeschool Cooperative is making in the community but also to support this program financially.

Thanks to Tiers Free, I've found academic success and the audacity to envision a life beyond my circumstances. Post-graduation, I aspire to find meaningful employment as an entrepreneur. Being an entrepreneur intrigues me because it gives me back the one thing that I never had in my entire life—control over what happens to me. Doubts linger, but they will not deter me. I've made a vow to transcend my challenges, to honor the journey, and to emerge victorious.

I am here not only to challenge the foster care-to-prison pipeline but to champion a cause.

This cause that I want to champion is a cause that is deeply personal to me. I want to champion the cause of change for how children enter the foster care system and how they are supported as they exit that system. As I stand here today, I also carry with me the weight of a fractured relationship with my mother and two brothers. It was a bond marked not by the warmth of maternal affection, but by a persistent sense of alienation. I grappled with feelings of betrayal, as promises made were seldom kept, and I often felt like an outsider even within the walls of my own home.

I watched as others were treated with a leniency I never received, their actions excused in a way that mine never were. It instilled in me a deep-seated sense of injustice, a feeling that I was held to a different standard, one that was unattainable and unfair.

The control my mother wielded was absolute, and despite the presence of a stepfather, it was clear who steered the ship of our family life. In my quest for something better, something that felt like hope, I began to run. Not away from challenges, but towards the possibility of a life where I was seen, heard, and valued.

Running became my protest, a silent scream for recognition, for a chance to prove that I deserved more than the hand I'd been dealt. It was a plea for a future where my aspirations wouldn't be suffocated by circumstances, where my potential could be nurtured rather than negated. In sharing this part of my story, I do not seek sympathy, but understanding. Understanding that the path I've walked is one that many foster children find themselves on, a path where the desire for love and stability is often met with disappointment and heartache.

But let this be clear: my past does not define me. It has shaped me, yes, but it is the strength I've found in overcoming these trials that truly characterizes who I am. It is the resilience I've honed, the determination I've fostered, and the unwavering belief in my own worth that has brought me to this podium today.

As I look towards the future, I see not a continuation of past struggles, but a horizon brimming with opportunity. I am ready to take the lessons learned from my experiences and channel them into creating a life of purpose and success.

Thank you for listening, for bearing witness to my journey, and for joining me in the fight to ensure that no child's future is predetermined by their beginnings.

2024 Cassius Bell
Macon County Graduation

Good afternoon, respected faculty, proud parents, and students. I'm Cassius Bell, and my journey to this moment is proof that our only limits are the ones we set for ourselves.

Growing up, school wasn't a smooth ride for me. I faced challenges ranging from bullying over my appearance to the discouraging feeling of being the oldest in my class. Yes, I was eighteen years old in the tenth grade, and trust me, my classmates never let me forget it. Their laughter trailed me everywhere, like a reminder of the uphill climb I had to face every day.

I decided to limit my school days to escape the constant reminders. But this decision came at a cost. It affected my grades, and when I did attend, I found myself lost in the lessons. I was failing all my classes, with the only exception being gym.

Another blow came when I was held back in the sixth grade for missing the last day of summer school. This delay meant I would graduate late, and change my career path. Had I been promoted, I would be a senior this year, on the brink of graduation, ready to spread my wings and take on the world.

And so, I was left behind. I became one of the casualties of a system that too often fails to recognize the unique struggles faced by students like myself. A fourteen-year study from 2008 to 2022 by the *Journal of Educational Psychology* showed that retaining a student in elementary school increased the probability that they would drop out of school.

You see, when students are held back, it sends a message that they're not good enough, that they don't measure up to their peers. And for many students, that message can be crushing.

Eventually, I reached a breaking point. I stopped attending school altogether, convinced that there was no hope for me. I was convinced that I was destined to become either a high school dropout or a late graduate. I felt like a nobody.

The thought of getting a GED crossed my mind, but I knew certain doors would remain closed with that route. Most of my family had a GED or dropped out of high school, but I was determined to break that cycle, to strive for more. I couldn't bear the thought of disappointing my mother and grandmother, of squandering the potential they saw in me.

I was scared I wouldn't finish this program on time and end up dropping out of high school. That fear haunted me. But amidst it all, I saw homeschooling as a safe option that could keep me out of trouble at school. I refused to accept defeat without a fight.

But beyond that, what truly motivated me was a promise I made to my mother. Before she passed away, she always asked about my dreams for the future, showing me endless possibilities that awaited me with a diploma in hand. I couldn't let her down.

And today, as I stand here, I know that fulfilling that promise is the greatest tribute I can give to her memory. But why stop here when there are so many possibilities ahead?

My main goal now is to secure a well-paying job and start saving up to leave Dawson behind. With determination and hard work, I believe I can achieve this dream. And who knows? Maybe with enough savings, I'll have the chance to pursue higher education and create an even brighter future for myself.

The key is to keep turning the pages and see where your dreams take you. Remember, you're not alone; there are people rooting for you. Reach out for help—to a counselor, a teacher, or a family member. Stay motivated, stay focused, and never lose sight of your goals. You've got what it takes to make it happen.

2024 Brittany Myers
Macon County Graduation

Good morning, distinguished guests, respected staff, and fellow graduates. My name is Brittany Myers. As I reflect on my journey, I realize that the difficulties I faced shaped me into the resilient person I am today.

Growing up, I always knew education was important. But for me, school felt more like a test of endurance than a place to explore new things. I had to learn information I was sure I'd never use, and some days, I just wanted to be anywhere but there.

The hardest part about school was waking up each morning. I

had to drag myself to a place that felt unwelcoming and suffer the monotonous routine. I remember battling with anxiety, depression, and the sheer exhaustion of keeping up with it all. I remember the struggle to maintain good grades and the constant battle to pass each test.

I felt the weight of the world on my shoulders and believed that I couldn't bear it any longer. My attendance dwindled, and eventually, I stopped showing up altogether.

But wait, my story didn't end there. It only ends when you give up. Instead, I picked myself up, dusted myself off, and decided to reclaim what I had left behind. I decided to enroll in GED. I studied for hours and I attended class every single chance I had. Then came the test and I failed. So I tried again and again but for the first time in my life the harder I worked towards the goal the further away from the goal I found myself.

That's the reality for a lot of us who have tried to get our GED in the past. I had honestly given up on graduating until I learned about the Macon County Chiefs' Diploma Program. I thought about enrolling in the program for years but I would always talk myself out of simply asking about the next steps.

But something changed for me in 2023. I wanted my high school diploma more than I wanted to remain paralyzed by fear. I had heard about the online classes and I knew it required a lot of preparation, dedication, and studying. But then the ghosts of my past started revisiting me. I was afraid I wouldn't accomplish a milestone I deeply longed for. There were moments when I questioned whether my role as a helping mother would be compromised by the hours spent on the computer.

I doubted myself for so many reasons, but I didn't let any of them stop me.

I persisted because I wanted to set an example for my children.

I wanted them to see that success is not handed to us but earned through relentless effort. And as I watch them grow, I know in my heart that they will remember their mother's journey. And they will know that they too can achieve anything they set their hearts on. I can hardly wait for that day!

But my journey doesn't end with graduation. My goal is to continue growing and giving back. I carry with me a burning passion for helping others. Whether it's as a teacher, a paraprofessional educator, a caregiver, or a tutor, I aspire to make a real difference in people's lives.

In the end, remember this: there's always time to play catch-up, but that doesn't mean you shouldn't strive to be a step ahead. Live fully in the moment, but remain mindful of your actions. Mistakes are inevitable. I've done my fair share, ones that left me feeling small and vulnerable. I was disappointed, angered, and sad all at once for not finishing high school the traditional way.

But I didn't let those mistakes dictate my future. I've let go of the disappointment and self-doubt that have plagued me for too long. Instead, I embrace the pride and sense of accomplishment that come with returning to complete my education.

So know that you are capable, you are valuable, and you are destined for greatness. Giving up leads to dead ends and regrets. Someday, you'll look back and wish you had seized the opportunities before you. Whatever challenges you're facing right now, push through them and keep your eyes on the end goal.

The journey may be tough, but the reward is beyond measure.

2024 Jasmine Bivins
Macon County Graduation Reflection Speech

Good afternoon, respected faculty, proud parents, and my fellow students.

I want to start off by congratulating all the graduates. My name is Jasmine Bivins. I am someone who refuses to be defined by my circumstances but by the strength I've found within myself.

From my early days in Head Start, pre-K, and elementary school, education was a source of joy and excitement. High school brought some of the best years of my life—a time so precious that I would trade anything to relive those moments once more.

Fast forward to my eleventh grade, as I was nearing the finish line. I became pregnant, and soon after, depression took hold of me. Suddenly, life wasn't all roses and rainbows anymore. The dreams I once held so close—college, career, the future I had meticulously planned—now seemed distant and unattainable.

It felt like the ground beneath me had shifted. It was like my legs gave out just before the final lap of a race. I wish I could have held on until the finish line, but I couldn't. Depression wrapped around me like a suffocating blanket, making it difficult to see the light at the end of the tunnel.

It wasn't the grades or the classes that challenged me; it was simply getting out of bed. What I was going through just seemed to overpower me—on top of being pregnant. But you know what? Even in my darkest moments, I'd think about what it would mean to walk across that stage and hold that diploma in my hands. I couldn't let go of that vision.

Since 2019, I have enrolled in not one but two different GED programs, both of which ended in disappointment. Then, I discovered this homeschool diploma program. It was like all the traffic lights had turned green at once, signaling a chance to start anew.

This program offered me the flexibility and support that I so desperately needed. I could work at my own pace, free from the constant pressure and nagging doubts that had plagued me before. It proved to be the light at the end of a very long, dark tunnel.

Fast forward to now, and here I am, standing on the brink of finally achieving what has felt elusive for so long. I've finally crossed that finish line.

With my high school diploma in hand, I dream of becoming a licensed cosmetologist and then furthering my education at Fort Valley State University to pursue a degree in social work. My goal is to become a social worker, to give back and help those in need.

But more than any career aspiration, I made a promise to myself. I promise to conquer every dream, to love myself unconditionally, and to do whatever it takes to succeed. It wasn't an easy promise to keep, but it was the most important one I ever made.

If I could travel back in time, I would encourage my past self to keep going. I would tell her, "You've got this! The victory is within reach, so don't you dare give up now." I would advise her to enjoy prom and participate in extracurricular activities like she always wanted. I would beg her not to let her mental health win and to fight against it with every ounce of strength she had.

But today, I've come to terms with all the things I couldn't do, the person I couldn't become, and the opportunities I've missed. Through it all, I've emerged stronger, wiser, and more resilient than ever before. I've faced my demons head-on and come out on top.

The bottom line is that delayed does not mean denied. It's natural to feel discouraged when things don't go according to plan. But it's important to remember that just because something is taking longer than expected doesn't mean it won't happen.

Remember, the start sets the scene, but the finish seals the story.

2024 Dottie
Macon County Rural Communities Diploma Program

Good afternoon, respected faculty, proud parents, and students. My name is Dottie, and I've learned that to succeed, you must be willing to push through the hardest moments, even when quitting seems like the easiest path.

I was in seventh grade when my life took a dramatic turn—I got pregnant. It took a toll on me, but I refused to let it derail my education. I continued to attend school throughout my junior high years. But just as I was finding my footing, I found myself pregnant once more, this time with a son.

By the time I entered high school, my responsibilities had multiplied, and so had the magnitude of my struggle.

During my entire ninth-grade year, I fought to stay on track. But in the tenth grade, I was completely overwhelmed. The hardest part of my school journey was balancing motherhood and education. It tore me apart to see my daughter cry every time I left for school. If only there had been another choice! It was a sacrifice we both had to make.

I pushed through to tenth grade, but it was a battle I couldn't win. Just one semester in, I felt like I was lost in the lessons, unable to find my way. I began to believe that school wasn't meant for me anymore. Desperate and defeated, I asked my mother if I could withdraw from school and attend GED classes.

Looking back, I see how my own struggles clouded my judgment. I realize I put our dreams on the line. I wasn't just giving up on school—I was giving up on the very idea of a better future for myself and my children.

Meanwhile, the art of doing hair became my true passion. I

learned to cut hair by practicing on my son's head until I perfected it. I started braiding hair at ten years old and have done all kinds of hairstyles since then.

But deep down, I knew I needed to catch up on my education. Having my kids so young made me fall behind in school, but my determination to provide a better life for them never wavered. So, I joined the TANF program. This program required me to attend GED classes or work forty hours a week at the bus station. I chose to pursue my GED.

However, the financial assistance from the TANF checks fell short in meeting our needs. At that point, I couldn't sit back and hope for miracles. So, I stopped attending GED classes and got a job. I worked hard and supported my children for a long time. There were no shortcuts, no easy solutions—just hard work and relentless persistence. Yet once again, I found myself at the doorstep of GED school, hoping for a different outcome. But the familiar struggle of balancing childcare and studies reared its head once more. The same challenges led me to the same conclusion. And once again, I quit, convinced that school just wasn't meant for someone like me.

Throughout the ups and downs of life, my desire to get a high school diploma never faded. For me, it was more than just a piece of paper; it was a symbol of hope, a ticket to a better future for both myself and my children. It was a promise of better job opportunities and a chance to break free from the cycle of struggle.

I enrolled in the Chiefs' Diploma Program, and you know what happened? I got kicked out not once, not twice, but three times. Yet, with each rejection, I dusted myself off and stood tall, refusing to let defeat define me.

Throughout it all, I would tell myself, "Dottie, you have to keep pushing forward. You know you're capable of so much more. So why keep rebelling against your own success?"

I promised myself not to let people down this time—people who believed in me. I could feel it in my bones, and they could see it in my eyes—I had the brain, the determination, and the courage to achieve this goal. I wanted something more from life—not just knowledge, but validation to prove my worth.

And today, it all came together. With a diploma in hand, I can enter any field I desire, knowing that my education is up to par. I stand tall and proud, ready to take on whatever challenges come my way. Because now I know that no matter how fierce the storm may rage, I have the strength to weather it and emerge stronger on the other side. To all of those who are listening: If I can get a diploma, so can you.

Believe in yourself, push your limits, and make it happen.

Crystal Spence, Parent Reflection of Program Impact
Tiers Free Academy Alternative Diploma Program

My daughter was in the eleventh grade and struggling at the time with the public school system. She had given up and was going to drop out with her only option to get a diploma being the GED at the adult literacy program. As I stood feeling helpless and venting to Dr. Mabry (or Doc as she's known in our family), she enlightened me on the option of homeschooling. This would have allowed my daughter to obtain an actual high school diploma. I didn't know a lot about homeschooling but it seemed like it would be complicated and it didn't seem feasible for us at the time. But that's where we learned about the Tiers Free Academy Alternative Diploma Program.

My daughter was nervous about doing school again at first because of her experience with the public school and another local alternative high school program. Public school began to fail my daughter as early as middle school. The classrooms were run by the students rather than the teachers. She was bullied to the point she began to struggle academically. It all ended up impacting her emotional health and she became depressed.

In the past I had tried local programs. For instance, there was one which cost us $75 a week. The only thing that my child got from there was unhealthy relationships with other unmotivated students who were as lost as she was. The other program seemed to be in place for the money more than the education and that ultimately failed my child too. When we finally decided to enroll with Dr. Mabry's program, we noticed differences right away. The biggest difference was that we had a lot of flexibility with the curriculum; it wasn't a one-size-fits-all approach. I watched my daughter's confidence soar as she finished her class each month. Even though all of the classes were online and she never physically sat in the classroom, Dr. Mabry was there with her every step of the way.

Her graduation day was the best part. I watched with my family as she received her high school diploma. It was presented to her in full cap and gown, which was ground-breaking for her self-esteem! This was the best news and immediately her life-altering journey began!

For other parents who find themselves in a similar situation, please step outside of your comfort zone and know that your child does not have to go through all the unnecessary stress destroying their confidence. Homeschool students can receive a real-life education without suffering the frustrations and inequalities of the public system. Homeschooling is not only equivalent to the standard public school education, it's flexible enough to be fun and effective enough to create a solid foundation enabling your child to thrive.

Using a program like Tiers Free Academy sends your child a few key messages they need in life. Not only does their family believe in them and their ability to succeed, but also that you all are refusing to settle for only a GED. These children are ripe and ready to receive the skills and mental acuity a fair education can offer and they deserve nothing less.

Dr. Annise Mabry saw a real need in our communities. Providing a scaffolding to the students who have no support in the public system, her academy can break through the educational barrier. It's the barrier that ultimately becomes an employment barrier and creates a vicious cycle of failure and crime. She is breaking that cycle each time she helps a high school dropout transform into a high school graduate. She is a quiet storm sending a real message by her actions to families and communities. Homes where students have given up on school and communities where leaders are ready to make real economic change ... they don't have to settle for academic programs that don't fit their needs or GED programs that have their own stigma. #EducationIsPower.

2024 Kaylin Driggers
Inaugural Graduation Reflection Speaker
Clarke County Rural Communities Diploma Program

Ladies and gentlemen, respected faculty, proud parents, and fellow graduates,

My name is Kaylin Driggers, and I am someone who has fought through life's battles to stand proudly before you today. I have accomplished what once seemed impossible at 27 years old with two kids. Growing up, I moved schools every single year. Each time, the adjustment got harder. Some schools were ahead of me academically, some were behind. Trying to keep up with topics I hadn't really learned yet was a major learning block for me. It felt like I was running a never-ending race where the finish line kept moving further away.

The constant adjustment took its toll, but nothing could prepare me for the horrific event that would change the trajectory of my life forever.

In 9th grade, my life took a harrowing turn. I was sexually assaulted at a house party. The trauma of that night was compounded by relentless bullying from some of my assailant's friends. It made unbearable for me to continue attending public school. The school environment became a place of dread and anxiety.

I begged my grandparents, who had custody of me, to not ever make me face those people again. Seeing how distressed I was, they decided to take me out of public school and homeschool me. But as a teenager, I didn't prioritize my education. With the freedom to sleep in, stay up late, go to the lake, and do anything else that caught my fancy, schoolwork quickly fell to the bottom of my list. I officially dropped out at 16, naively thinking I didn't need a diploma.

It wasn't until I was 18 and pregnant with my daughter that I realized the magnitude of my mistake. Over the years, my dream career changed multiple times—from cosmetology to nursing, to veterinary medicine, and back to cosmetology. Each time, I was held back by the same thing: not having a high school diploma.

Yet, I wasn't alone in this struggle. Across America, over twenty-seven million adults aged twenty-five or older face the same barrier—a missing credential, high school diploma, or GED—that locks them out of nearly eighty percent of job opportunities in this country. In Georgia alone, there are 866,000 adults, just like me, without high school diplomas.

I didn't want to be part of such statistics.

I attended two different GED schools over the years, each time coming so close to finishing yet never quite reaching the finish line.

The daily juggle of raising two young children while working to support them was overwhelming. Slowly, I began to resign myself to the belief that perhaps achieving any form of diploma was simply beyond my grasp.

Starting my education again came with a lot of fear—fear of being judged for my age, fear of not measuring up, and fear of the impossible task of balancing the demands of my children, school, and work.

But this time, I chose to rise above my fears. This time, I resolved to let nothing, not even my deepest anxieties, dictate my path. This is by far the best thing I've ever done. With the support of my children, grandparents, mother, stepfather, and boyfriend, I pushed through. I made a promise to myself to always push through, no matter how hard it got. I promised to persevere through homelessness, financial struggles, and the tough challenge of raising my kids alone. I told myself to let go of what weighed me down. I realized the mountains I carried were only meant to be climbed.

And today, I stand on the edge of realizing that promise. My grand- parents will witness my graduation—the first in our family since their time. My children will see resilience in my actions and what it means to overcome. And me? I've found a deep, unshakable pride in myself, a pride earned through every struggle faced and every promise kept.

This achievement opens doors I didn't realize were closed. Yet it's only the beginning. After graduating, I plan to pursue cosmetology. This program has given me the confidence to continue my education and pursue my dream career. I want to show my kids that if I can do it, they can too. That, they really have to work for what they want in life, it's more than just keeping your faith or not giving up.

To anyone facing similar battles, I request you to take a deep breath and hold on. Dropping out may seem like a quick fix, but take a moment to think about what that decision means for your future. A diploma is far more than a piece of paper; it's your ticket to get jobs easier, have more opportunities to advance in career, and get to experience college.

If I could turn back time, I'd tell my younger self, "Things get better." The feeling of being overwhelmed is temporary, but a diploma lasts a lifetime, and the effort you put in now will pay off for years to come. And guess what? It's worth every bit of it.

So, don't let fear hold you back. Remember, nothing worth having ever comes easy. Embrace the struggle and hold on through the tough times. Your future self will look back with gratitude for pushing through.

Thank you, and congratulations to us all!

Appendix B
Homeschool Pro Tips: The Stuff I Wish I Knew When I Started

Homeschool Pro Tip: Position for a learning pivot.

The first year of homeschooling, I was determined to get everything right. I attended every homeschool conference and workshop I could find, hoping to gain all the knowledge I needed to succeed. But instead of feeling empowered, I often walked away feeling inadequate. As a single parent homeschooling my children without a support system, I felt out of place. We weren't a "career homeschool family"—my children had been in public school before this. So, when the carefully curated curriculum I had invested in didn't work, I felt like I had failed.

But the truth was, I hadn't failed. What I had done was put myself in a box, not allowing any space for the necessary learning pivots.

If you've chosen to homeschool, you've made that decision for a reason. As a homeschool parent, your role is that of a learning facilitator. This means you're there to facilitate—not direct—the learning process. When you take on this role, it opens up the flexibility you and your child need to pivot and adjust as often as necessary. Homeschooling isn't about rigidly sticking to a plan; it's about creating an environment where learning can evolve naturally, adapting to your child's needs and interests.

Homeschool Pro Tip: Build learning confidence first. Focus on content mastery second.

When I started homeschooling my daughter, she was in the eighth grade, but she was reading at a college level. The grade-level work felt tedious and frustrating for her because it didn't challenge her intellect. On the other hand, my son presented a different challenge. He was in the fourth grade, but his reading skills were at a second-grade level. What I eventually learned about homeschooling was that my children's public school grade level might not align with their actual content mastery level.

Despite my son's struggle with reading, his confidence in his ability to learn was low, but his motivation to engage in the learning process remained high. He hadn't been completely broken down by the academic system, which gave me the opportunity to build up his learning confidence first. By focusing on building his confidence, I could create a foundation where he felt empowered to improve his skills and take on new challenges.

This experience taught me that homeschooling isn't just about meeting academic benchmarks; it's about understanding where your child is in their learning journey and meeting them there. It's about fostering a sense of confidence and a love for learning, which often requires tailoring the educational experience to fit their unique needs.

Homeschool Pro Tip: Design your own student support team.

It's homeschool not alone school. You can't do this alone.

You need to create a support team for yourself and your child. You are not an expert in all things. For example, math and science are not my strong areas. Could I teach these classes to my child? Yes, I could, but doing so wouldn't create an optimal learning experience for either of us. That's why using homeschool cooperatives is essential. I also hired private tutors to give my child in-depth learning support. When I took the role of learning facilitator rather than primary educator, I felt a true relief and I could finally breathe.

Homeschool Pro Tip: Buy used curriculum.

When you are homeschooling, you have to give yourself permission to change curriculum midstream. That's why I encourage parents who want to buy curriculum to always buy used—never buy new because you don't know if it is going to work for your child. The first year we homeschooled, I attended every homeschool conference and workshop I could find. I spent over $800 on the Shiller Math curriculum. We used it twice and I quickly realized it was not a good fit for us. I finally sold it for $400 and took that as my lesson to never buy new again. I truly think our game changer moment came with not only finding the right tutors but also the right curricula. When you have a child who struggles with the foundational concepts of reading, English Language Arts (ELA) is always a challenge. Some of the best ELA curricula I have used with my son are Explode the Code, Learning Without Tears, Red Hot Root Words, and SpellWell.

Homeschool Pro Tip: Leverage dual enrollment classes for high school students.

Parents are always intrigued by how I was able to get a tenth-grade student into dual enrollment classes. The truth is, in Georgia it's easy. Granted, I didn't push for dual enrollment at a university, nor do I ever encourage parents who work with me to send their homeschooled children to the major universities for dual enrollment. Rather, I encourage parents in Georgia to look at technical colleges because all technical colleges in our state have two-by-two agreements with Georgia universities. A two-by-two agreement simply means that if a student completes two years at one location, then upon graduation he or she is guaranteed admission into the partner location. In states that have community or junior colleges, these two-by-two agreements are very similar in nature.

Homeschool Pro Tip: Facilitate learning that fosters independence.

Homeschool students by nature are familiar with independent learning. For example, when we attended in-person classes, my son would go to his English/Language Arts class only once a week for one hour. Then, he spent the remaining four weekdays working on assignments. This roughly translates to taking a Monday/Wednesday college class—he is prepared to complete work for that class every day rather than just on class days. This is what homeschool looks like: we design a schedule that works for us and fits into our lives. Then we make a commitment to the process.

We participated in our last in-person homeschool cooperative class in 2020 and my son graduated in 2021. He is now in his last year of technical college where he is studying Aviation Maintenance.

Many people see me now but few understand those early days when I was alone and desperately searching for resources and ultimately a tribe. I found both because I never gave up—what I was fighting for was so much greater than what I was fighting against.

Homeschool Pro Tip: Keep all of your records.

Your homeschool records are your responsibility. Even if you use a homeschool cooperative that keeps records for you, it is still your responsibility as a homeschool parent to keep your own records. Tiers Free Homeschool Cooperative houses all of our homeschool records with Parchment.com. Parents always get so excited about their child getting a high school diploma. Diplomas are great but it's the documentation (transcript) that allows the child to get the diploma that matters.

Appendix C
The Plain Language Homeschool Checklist

Creating a homeschooling checklist can help parents make informed decisions and ensure they are well-prepared to start homeschooling. Here's a comprehensive checklist for parents considering homeschooling:

Pre-Decision Checklist
Research State Laws and Requirements:
- Understand homeschooling laws and regulations in your state or country.
- Determine necessary notifications or registrations with educational authorities.

Assess Your Family's Needs:
- Consider your child's learning style, needs, and interests.
- Evaluate your family's schedule, financial situation, and available resources.

Evaluate Your Commitment:
- Reflect on your ability to dedicate time and effort to homeschooling.
- Consider the impact on your family's lifestyle and daily routine.

Explore Homeschooling Methods and Philosophies:

- Research different approaches such as Classical, Montessori, Charlotte Mason, Unschooling, etc.
- Identify which philosophy aligns with your educational values and goals.

Connect with Homeschooling Communities:

- Join local or online homeschooling groups for support and resources.
- Attend homeschooling events or workshops to gain insights and advice.

Planning and Preparation
Set Educational Goals:

- Define short-term and long-term academic and personal development goals for your child.
- Identify skills and knowledge you want your child to acquire.

Choose a Curriculum:

- Research and select a curriculum that suits your educational philosophy and goals.
- Consider a mix of textbooks, online resources, and experiential learning.

Create a Learning Space:

- Designate a comfortable, organized, and distraction-free area for homeschooling.
- Ensure it has necessary supplies, such as desks, chairs, and educational materials.

Plan a Daily and Weekly Schedule:

- Establish a flexible yet consistent routine for learning and activities.
- Include time for academics, arts, physical activities, and socialization.

Gather Resources and Materials:
- Purchase or gather textbooks, workbooks, and other learning materials.
- Explore educational apps, websites, and local library resources.

Implementation
Establish a Record-Keeping System:
- Keep track of attendance, progress, and completed assignments.
- Maintain records of assessments, projects, and extracurricular activities.

Develop Assessment Methods:
- Plan regular evaluations to assess your child's progress and understanding.
- Use a variety of methods, such as quizzes, projects, and presentations.

Foster a Supportive Learning Environment:
- Encourage curiosity, creativity, and independent learning.
- Provide positive reinforcement and celebrate achievements.

Incorporate Socialization Opportunities:
- Arrange playdates, field trips, and group activities with other homeschoolers.

- Involve your child in community events, clubs, or sports teams.

Review and Adjust:
- Regularly review your homeschooling approach and make adjustments as needed.
- Seek feedback from your child and be open to changes for improvement.

Ongoing Support and Growth
Stay Informed and Inspired:
- Continue learning about new homeschooling methods and resources.
- Attend homeschooling conferences and read relevant books and articles.

Seek Professional Support if Needed:
- Consider hiring tutors or enrolling in online courses for specific subjects.
- Consult educational professionals if your child requires special assistance.

Reflect and Recharge:
- Take breaks and vacations to prevent burnout for both you and your child.
- Reflect on the homeschooling journey and celebrate milestones together.

Acknowledgements

To the resilient and courageous students who refuse to be limited by systems that were never built for them—your defiance is the spark of change.

To the parents, guardians, and educators who believe in the transformative power of individualized education and stand unwavering in their commitment to a child's unique path—you are the true architects of a better tomorrow.

And to every child who dares to dream beyond the boundaries of traditional learning—you are the revolution.

To my editors, Stephanie Wilson and Magdalena Bartkowska—thank you for your keen insights, unwavering support, and for bringing clarity to this vision.

In loving memory of my grandfather, my father, and Mrs. Becky Wood—whose legacy of strength, resilience, and quiet wisdom continues to guide me every day. This work is for you.

www.ingramcontent.com/pod-product-compliance
Lightning Source LLC
Chambersburg PA
CBHW052210090526
44584CB00016BA/2048